Frances Bickford
Feb. 4 1971
Singapore

# MALAY CUSTOMS
## and
# TRADITIONS

By
ALWI BIN SHEIKH ALHADY

DONALD MOORE PRESS LTD
Singapore

*First published in Singapore, 1962*
*by* DONALD MOORE *for*
*EASTERN UNIVERSITIES PRESS, LTD.*
*Reprinted 1967*
*by Donald Moore Press Ltd*

© 1962, ALWI BIN SHEIKH ALHADY

Printed by Ho Printing Co., Singapore.

# FOREWORD

It is with great pleasure that I welcome the publication of this work on Malay customs and traditions and I congratulate its author, Tuan Syed Alwi bin Sheikh Alhady, on his diligence in compiling this book, which I believe is greatly needed, especially today, not only by Malays but also by those non-Malays who have settled in the Malay Peninsula and who desire to know what the customs and traditions of the Malays really are. As far as I know, this is the first time that such a book has been published, and I believe that it will be well received and widely read.

To write on Malay customs and traditions is by no means an easy task. Although the aims of similar traditions are generally the same in every Malay region, there are, in actual practice, some differences in usage and procedure. These differences must be taken into account, and it would be misleading to say that one practice is wrong and another is right, for as a Malay proverb says: *"Lain lubok lain ikan-nya"* or *"Lain padang lain belalang"*, which means that each region has its own distinctive customs and traditions.

Another difficulty which faces the writer on

Malay customs and traditions is the lack of any written information on the subject. So, anyone desiring to write on this theme is obliged to do a good deal of research, and to interview very elderly persons who know and still remember something about these practices — and there are not many such persons alive today. The problem arises chiefly because the customs and traditions of the Malays have been handed down from father to son, or from the old to the young, by word of mouth only, and not in written form.

Every nation holds fast to its own customs and traditions since it is by them that one nation is identified and differentiated from another, and since these practices show its way and view of life. This is so true of the Malays that they have a proverb which says: *"Biar mati anak, jangan mati 'adat"* (meaning: "We would prefer to lose a child than lose a custom"). Although this is so, yet it cannot be said that customs and traditions are unchanging or unchangeable, for anything of such a nature, if made unchangeable, would not last but would die out by itself. But changes should be made suitably and constructively, not destructively. Usually, they do not take place overnight, but by degrees over long periods, until they eventually become approved and accepted *'adat* or customs.

Before I end this brief foreword, I wish to take the opportunity to state that the royal customs and traditions that have been adopted and are practised in the State of Johore, and which are mentioned in this book, originated in Rhio, but that the articles of regalia, some of which are shown in illustrations in this book, were all made in Johore, nearly one hundred years ago, i.e. during the reign of Almarhum Sultan Abu Bakar ibni Almarhum Temenggong Ibrahim, and renewed, from time to time, during the reign of Almarhum Sultan Ibrahim ibni Almarhum Sultan Abu Bakar, who died on the 1st day of *Zulkaedah* in the year of the *Hijrah* 1378 (8th of May, 1959).

Lastly, I wish to mention here that Tuan Syed Alwi bin Sheikh Alhady, the author of this book, is one who was brought up in infancy in Rhio, and received his primary Malay education in the school there, and he did not leave for the Malay Peninsula until he was thirteen years old. As a child he saw the *'adat isti 'adat* adopted and practised in Rhio. These he still remembers and describes in this book.

ISMAIL BIN ABU BAKAR,
Dato' Penghulu Isti'adat,
Johore.

Johore Bahru,
22nd *Ra'al-awal*, 1379.
(25th September, 1959)

# CONTENTS

| | Page |
|---|---|
| FOREWORD | iii |
| LIST OF PLATES | ix |
| INTRODUCTION | xi |

## PART ONE
## *General Malay Customs & Traditions*

*Chapter*

| | | |
|---|---|---|
| I. | HOUSEHOLD AND KAMPONG CUSTOMS<br>A. Household Customs<br>B. Kampong or Mukim Customs | 3 |
| II. | PIERCING OF EAR-LOBES, CIRCUMCISION AND CHILDBIRTH<br>A. Piercing of Ear-lobes<br>B. Circumcision<br>C. Childbirth and Delivery | 7 |
| III. | MARRIAGE CUSTOMS<br>A. Marriage of a Maiden<br>B. Marriage of a Widow | 22 |
| IV. | FUNERAL CUSTOMS | 52 |

## CONTENTS

## PART TWO

## *Royal Malay Customs & Traditions*

*Chapter*             *Page*

I. LANGUAGE, ETIQUETTE AND ANCIENT LAWS    61
     A. Language Traditionally used for Royalty
     B. Dress Regulations
     C. Etiquette of Paying Homage to Royalty
     D. Prohibition Against Imitating the Structure of Certain Parts of the Palace
     E. Etiquette on Public Roads
     F. Duties and Responsibilities of the Penghulu Istana
     G. Duties and Responsibilities of the Penghulu Balairong Seri
     H. The right to eat together from the same tray

II. THE NOBAT (Royal Band)    78

III. RULES GOVERNING MARRIAGE    87
     A. Dowry and Expenses
     B. Order of the Royal Wedding Procession

IV. TABALKAN (INSTALLATION OF A MONARCH)    94
     The Oath of Loyalty

V. DEMISE AND FUNERAL OF A RULING MONARCH    117

*Appendix*
     A Brief Biography of Engku Mai    127

# LIST OF PLATES

*(between Pages 126 and 127)*

*Plate*

1. TONGKAT PENGHULU ISTANA (Ceremonial Staff for Palace Penghulu)
2. PEDANG KERAJAAN (Sword of State)
3. CHOGAN (Standard)
4. PEDANG KERAJAAN (Sword of State)
5. WALI (Ceremonial Shoulder-cloth)
6. SELENDANG (Ceremonial Sash)
7. KAIN-DUKONG (Ceremonial Neck-cloth)
8. TETAMPAN (Ceremonial Shoulder-cloth)
9. LEMBING AND TOMBAK (Spear)
10. PAYONG UBOR-UBOR (Royal Ceremonial Umbrellas)
11. PUAN (Betel-bowl)
12. TEPAK SIREH (Sireh-box)
13. ENGKU MAI

# INTRODUCTION

At the outset I wish to state that I do not claim that what I have written on Malay customs and traditions in this small book is complete in every detail, but I made this attempt to the best of my ability, knowledge and endeavour after many months of research. I sincerely hope that the information I have given is at least sufficient to serve as a guide, and as a basis for future research.

I dared to make the attempt to write on this subject because, in the first place, I still remember the customs and traditions practised by the Malays generally, and by Malay royalty particularly, in Rhio.

I was born in 1895 and I was brought up in Rhio until I reached the age of thirteen years, when I was taken by my father to Singapore to study the English language. Before that, I was, for over three years, a student in the Malay school in Pulau Penyengat, Rhio. As my father was the adopted son of Almarhum Raja Haji Ali Kelana ibni Almarhum Sultan Muhammad Yusoff, who was brother of the then Sultan Abdul Rahman of Rhio, our family was always in close contact with the royal household of the Sultan and, more particularly, with that of his brother. Our own house was situated just a stone's throw from the Sultan's palace and about a quarter of a mile from the palace of his brother, Almarhum Raja Haji Ali Kelana. So I naturally spent a good deal of my time daily at both the *Istana,* especially during ceremonial occasions, and saw how the *'adat isti-'adat* were carried out.

Secondly, I knew that there were still some old persons of Rhio about, and scraps of written matter on the subject available, and so for two months, during April and May, 1959, I did some research, interviewing venerable personages of Rhio in Singapore, Johore, and Selangor, and obtaining from them the necessary information to refresh, complement, and correct what I vaguely remembered on the subject.

To the following persons, therefore, I shall ever remain grateful for the very substantial and helpful information they gave me on the subject:

1. Yang Mulia Raja Muhammad Ariff (Engku Chik) bin Raja Mahmud of Rhio, now in Singapore, who lent me from thirty to forty hand-written pages of a script, written by the late *Yang Di-Pertuan Muda* of Rhio Lingga and re-copied finally by Raja Ali ibni Almarhum Raja Haji Ismail of Rhio at Pulau Penyengat on the 3rd day of *Safar,* 1361 (*Hijrah*) — 18th February, 1942.

2. Yang Mulia Raja Chik bin Omar of Rhio, now in Johore Bahru, for his advice and help, given at an interview, on certain points of doubt.

3. Lastly — but most important of all, Yang Mulia the venerable Raja Maimunah binti Raja Hassan, popularly known as "Engku Mai", whose picture and short biography, I have the honour, with her permission, to publish. From her information I was able to correct a number of important points and in addition she gave me seven loose leaves of a hand-written script on the Malay *'adat isti'adat*.

We very often hear, nowadays, through speeches delivered from platforms and over the air, and we read in articles in newspapers and magazines, strong promptings to uphold and safeguard the culture of our nation. Yet I believe that we should first know well the fundamentals of our national customs and traditions before we can rightly and safely uphold and safeguard our culture. This belief of mine, together with the encouragement of a few of my intimate friends, has been the strongest factor urging me to write this small book.

Readers please note that the term *'Adat Resam Melayu*, the title of PART ONE of this book, refers to the customs generally adopted and practised by the Malays of the Malay Peninsula (excepting those in Negri Sembilan and Malacca, who adopt and practise the *'adat perpateh*). The term *'Adat Isti'adat Diraja* in PART TWO, refers to the customs and traditions of Malay royalty in particular, and these are mostly practised only during royal ceremonial occasions. The regulations governing these were finally reviewed and revised in the reign of Sultan Sulaiman Badrul 'Alam Shah, *Sultan* and *Yang Di-Pertuan Besar* of Rhio and its dependencies. They have since been accepted by the Malays as their standard royal customs and traditions — just as Rhio Malay has been accepted as their standard language — and since the year of the *Hijrah* 1134, they have been widely adopted and practised, especially in Rhio, Johore, Selangor, and Pahang.

But as is true of almost all old habits, so it is of customs and traditions, that the passage of time brings with it many changes, and even renders some practices impracticable. This is especially so for the modern urban Malays, but, by and large, most of the rural Malays hold fast to their customs and traditions.

Lastly I wish to make special mention that I would not have been able to include illustrations of the articles of royal regalia in the book, had I not had the gracious and special permission of His Highness Sir Ismail ibni Almarhum Sultan Ibrahim, the *Sultan* of Johore, to take the pictures of some of the Johore State regalia in the *Istana Besar* at Johore Bahru, for no such collection is available anywhere else in the Peninsula. To His Highness, therefore, I shall ever remain grateful.

To Mr. Donald Moore is due my grateful thanks, for it was entirely at his suggestion that I made this my first venture to write a book in the English language. This is the English version of the book which I wrote in Romanised Malay and which has been published by the *Dewan Bahasa* and *Pustaka* of the Federation of Malaya.

In closing I beg to render my deepest thanks to the Hon'ble Dato' Ismail bin Abu Bakar, *Dato' Penghulu Isti'adat* of the State of Johore, for his help and co-operation, and above all for his trouble and goodness in going through the manuscript and in writing a preface for it; and no less do I thank the Hon'ble Dato' Syed Abdul Kadir bin Muhammad Bin-Yahaya, Captain Wan Rahim, and Colonel Musa bin Yusoff, all of Johore, for their encouragement, help, advice and co-operation — May Allah bless them all.

ALWI BIN SHEIKH ALHADY

Penang, 14th September, 1959.

# PART ONE

## GENERAL MALAY CUSTOMS & TRADITIONS

### 'ADAT RESAM MELAYU

CHAPTER ONE

# HOUSEHOLD AND KAMPONG CUSTOMS

Like all other nations in the world, the Malays have their own customs and traditions to follow or be bound by, and I shall attempt, as best I can, to explain briefly how these have been practised for many generations, although some of them have undergone changes with the passage of time and with altered world conditions.

## A. 'ADAT BERSERUMAH-TANGGA
(HOUSEHOLD CUSTOMS)

1. All members of a Malay household, especially the children, are strictly bound by the *'adat resam* to look upon the father and mother of the family as leaders and benefactors. Therefore unquestioned loyalty and obedience must be given to them, and all the respect due to them must be shown in daily acts and behaviour. For example, when a son is sent for by either of his parents, he should come to answer the call properly dressed, and with his cap on his head (except, of course, if he is too young a child for the imposition of the

*'adat*). In former days, it was considered highly insulting if a son came before his parents with a cigarette in his mouth — even though he were old enough himself to be a father. When in the presence of his parents, a man must behave with due respect. He should not, for example, cross his legs when sitting on a chair. Nor should he sit with one knee up, when resting on the floor. It was even more incumbent upon a daughter to behave gently and respectfully towards her parents. Similarly, a younger person must respect his or her elders. (Unfortunately this *'adat* is fast disappearing in practice particularly among the urban and modern Malays, who have been too much influenced by Western manners.)

2. It is customary (*di-'adatkan*) among the Malays, that as soon as a family comes to know of any of the following happenings in any one of the neighbouring families or households, either the head, or one or more members of the family, should go to visit the household in question to see if anything can be done to help or, in the case of misfortune, to relieve them:

   (a) If a newcomer has just moved in to stay with the neighbour
   (b) If illness or an accident befalls the neighbour
   (c) If someone in the house dies.

3. It has been laid down for generations in the *'adat resam Melayu* that between neighbours there

should exist good brotherly relations, peace and tranquillity; and that every member of each family should do his or her best to refrain from any act or word that may cause misunderstanding, or lead to quarrels, or give rise to feelings of enmity.

4. The Malay ʻ*adat* requires that every visitor to a Malay house be properly dressed. He is required by the ʻ*adat* to take off his footwear and leave it outside before entering. In the case of a female Malay visitor she should also, on entering a house, either take off her *kain kelumbong* (a second *sarong* used as a head-covering) or let it fall to her waist, gathering the folds over one arm (*berkemban*).

5. It is also provided in the Malay ʻ*adat* that a visitor (provided he does not come too late in the night) be at least offered some light refreshment or (for women particularly) *sa-kapor sireh* (preparation of *sireh* leaves) as a token of hospitality.

## B. ʻADAT BERSEKAMPONG
### (KAMPONG OR MUKIM CUSTOMS)

1. It has been traditionally observed as an ʻ*adat resam Melayu* that the residents of a *kampong* or *mukim* (district round a mosque), particularly the menfolk, should be in close contact with the *ketua kampong* or *penghulu mukim* so that their welfare may the more conveniently receive his attention.

2. Although it is already provided for in the tenets of the religion of Islam, it is also in the *'adat bersekampong* that every Malay or Muslim should attend the weekly congregational Friday Prayer at the *kampong* or *mukim* mosque.

3. Residents of a Malay *kampong* or *mukim*, as far as possible, are expected to work for the general welfare of the inhabitants, in the old system of *bergotong-royong* (mutual assistance).

4. They are also enjoined at least to visit, and preferably to help, as best they can, in any case of death, illness or misfortune in any of the neighbouring *kampong* or *mukim*.

5. The head of a household or family new to a district should at his earliest convenience make a report of his family's presence to the *ketua kampong* or *penghulu mukim*, and, if he is a Muslim, he should also inform the *siak* (caretaker) of the mosque. Likewise it is provided in the *'adat* that the *ketua* or *penghulu* and other residents of note should come, at least once, to pay the newcomer a visit of welcome.

CHAPTER TWO

# PIERCING OF EAR-LOBES, CIRCUMCISION, AND CHILDBIRTH

In this chapter I shall briefly explain three traditional ceremonies — one for adults and two for children — formerly widely practised by both urban and rural Malays, at great expense, simply because they were 'adat. Nowadays, fortunately, they are not so widely observed, least of all by urban Malays. These 'adat may very soon be dispensed with by Malays, and it is not a matter to be regretted if they are, from the point of view of economy.

These ceremonies accompany the events of:
- A. *Bertindek Telinga* (Piercing a hole in each lobe of a young girl's ears)
- B. *Bersunat* (Circumcision of a boy— optional, though preferred by Islam)
- C. *Beranak* (Giving birth or delivery).

## A. BERTINDEK TELINGA
(PIERCING OF EAR-LOBES)

This custom of ceremonial piercing of the ear-lobes must have originated long before the

Malays became Muslims. The ear-lobe piercing is only done to girls between five and ten years old. The actual operation does not take more than a few seconds, but the ceremony accompanying it may take at least half a day. After the guests, close relatives and neighbours, as well as friends of the parents, have arrived, the *kenduri* (quasi-religious feast) begins with a *jamuan* of rice and curry. At the end of the feasting, a *do'a* (prayer) is read by a *lebai* (lower order of priest) or an *'alim* (religious scholar), and after the *do'a*, all the guests disperse. The piercing is performed either before or after the *kenduri*. A woman simply pierces the lobe with a type of thorn, and this operation takes only a few seconds.

### B. BERSUNAT
(CIRCUMCISION)

This *'adat*, though not nowadays much practised by educated Malays or by those in urban areas, is still widely upheld by the more conservative Malays, especially in the *kampong*.

The circumcision ceremony is briefly as follows:

1. When a boy is about eight to twelve years old, his parents fix the date for his circumcision. Then invitations, either by letter or word of mouth, are sent out to near relatives, neighbours and friends of the parents — the number invited sometimes reaching three digits, and not rarely four digits! In the afternoon or evening before the day of the

actual circumcision, the boy is made ready, as a bridegroom is, for the ceremony. His hair is trimmed (*berandam*), he is dressed in gay and gleaming garments and then seated on a specially-made *pelamin* (bridal couch) before the gathering of guests, male and female. Before being put on the *pelamin* it is not unusual for him to be taken in procession through the town or village.

Furthermore, if the boy to be circumcised has completed learning to read all the thirty chapters of the Holy Quran, the circumcision ceremony is often preceded by the ceremony for *khatam Quran* (having finished learning to read the whole of the Quran), and takes place after the procession. The boy is placed in front of the *pelamin*, where he reads the verses in the last chapter of the Quran before the quests. After the reading, the boy kisses the hand first of his Quran teacher, and then of his parents, and then of the rest of the guests. He then sits on the *pelamin* for a while, and finally, descends for the feast. The guests present then join in the grand *jamuan* (feast), after which they are each presented with a *bunga telor* (ceremonial egg, dyed red and impaled on a stick topped with paper flowers).

Thus ends the first part of the ceremony.

2. The second part of the ceremony, which is the actual performance of the circumcision, takes place very early the next morning, when the boy to be circumcised is asked to take a thorough bath, and to wait until the *mudim* (the man who cir-

cumcises) arrives. The following materials for use in the ceremony are made ready for the *mudim*:

(i) Two or three yards of white cloth
(ii) One live cock
(iii) One big jug or bowl of water
(iv) One stem of a banana tree
(v) One *sireh*-box or a plate with *sireh* and all its ingredients
(vi) Money, amounting to three dollars or more as *pengkeras* (payment for services rendered), put in the *sireh*-box or a plate for the *mudim*.

As soon as the *mudim* arrives, he takes the boy from his bath and bathes him with the water from the bowl (after he has read some spell or *jampi* over it), while the boy stands on the top rung, or step, of a stairway. Then the *mudim* leads him to the banana tree stem, and makes him sit astride it. After preparing the boy's penis for the operation, the *mudim* then as fast as lightning, cuts off the stretched end of the foreskin. Immediately after this operation, the *mudim* takes the live cock and pushes its head towards the boy's penis once or twice, and notes the response of the cock; should the feathers round the cock's neck puff out when it comes close to the penis, it is traditionally believed to be an omen showing that the boy will be highly sexed, liable to marry more than once, or to be polygamous. The *mudim* then dresses the wound and that ends the ceremony of circumcision.

The white cloth, the cock, and the *sireh*-box with the money go to the *mudim* as gifts for services rendered, and the *mudim* comes daily for three days to nurse the boy, after which his work and responsibilities end.

3. There is one more point worth mentioning here, that is a practice of *kampong* Malays of former days, which was connected with circumcision, and which was looked upon as an *'adat* and widely adopted. It was the custom of letting the boy, from infancy, keep one or two, or sometimes even three, *jambul* or *bocheng* (tufts of hair, uncut or unshaved) either on the crown or back of his head, until the day of circumcision, when the *jambul* or *bocheng* would be shaved off. But this practice has long since been discarded, for no Malay boy who has been rightly enlightened by education, cares to be adorned with such *bocheng*.

Allah be praised, today this ceremonial circumcision is no longer looked upon or practised as an *'adat* even by the *kampong* Malays. They have now made the best use of the services of the medical clinics and hospitals, and found them to be very much more economical, healthier, and safer, and thus this old practice is fast disappearing from even the rural areas in the Malay Peninsula.

NOTE

The circumcision of girls is an age-old Malay practice which is still prevalent today. Malays believe, or were made to believe, that it is *sunnah* (commendable but not obligatory in Islam) to circumcise girls as well. God knows from where they get such a tenet! I am sorry, but I, for one, entirely disagree with and dissociate myself from such a belief, and I consider the operation, done to a girl, most unreasonable and cruel. Thus, what I have said above on the subject of circumcision concerns ONLY THE CIRCUMCISION OF BOYS.

## C. BERSALIN AND BERANAK
(CHILDBIRTH AND DELIVERY)

The customary practices in the 'adat of *bersalin* (childbirth or delivery) have for the last thirty or forty years undergone a great deal of change for the better, but the old ways are still being widely practised by most of the rural people. The following are traditional practices, in six stages from the completion of the seventh month of pregnancy:

1. *Lenggang* or *kirim perut* (rocking the abdomen and engaging a midwife)
2. Actual delivery
3. Shaving and naming of the baby
4. The mother in the period of taboo
5. Bathing of the mother after the taboo period
6. *Kenduri Lepas Pantang* (quasi-religious ceremonial feast after taboo).

1. LENGGANG PERUT (Rocking of the Abdomen)

The term *lenggang perut* (rocking of the abdomen) is mostly used by the Malays in the southern states of Malaya, while the term *kirim perut* with the same meaning and significance is widely used by the Malays of the northern states of the Peninsula. The former is the right term and denotes the ceremonies carried out for a prospective mother completing her seventh month of pregnancy.

A midwife or *bidan,* agreed upon, is called to examine the mother-to-be, and when it is ascertained that she has truly completed the seventh month of her pregnancy, the midwife is then *di-tempah* (engaged to perform the forthcoming delivery). The materials to be made ready for the ceremonial performance of the *lenggang perut* and engagement of the midwife, are as follows:

(i) Seven *sarong,* preferably of seven different colours
(ii) One *gantang* (Malay gallon) of raw rice
(iii) One ripe coconut with its husk completely peeled off
(iv) Some raw cotton yarn
(v) One stick of *damar* (resin or gum)
(vi) Some candles
(vii) One *sireh*-box or plate, complete with all its ingredients

- (viii) *Pengkeras* (fee for services rendered) of five quarters (one dollar and twenty-five cents) to be placed in the *sireh*-box or a plate
- (ix) A little coconut oil or massage oil in a small cup or saucer.

The *bidan* then comes and starts to perform the ceremonies required by the '*adat resam* of *melenggang perut*.

(a) The *bidan* first spreads the seven different coloured *sarong* lengthwise (one on top of another) on a mattress, and the pregnant wife lies down on them. Then the midwife slowly massages the woman's abdomen with the oil, from below the chest downwards, for a little while. After this the *bidan* takes the peeled coconut and rolls it slowly down the abdomen of the wife, seven times over. On the seventh occasion the coconut is allowed to roll down by itself from the abdomen to the floor. The *bidan* follows the coconut to note its position when it stops rolling. If it stops with its "eyes" pointing upwards it is believed that the woman will give birth to a boy, if downwards, to a girl.

(b) After that the *bidan* starts the actual act of *melenggang perut* (rocking the abdomen) by grasping each end of the topmost *sarong* in either hand and lifting the body thus cradled, just a little. After rocking it to left and right once or twice, she pulls the *sarong* out from under the body of the mother-to-be. It is from this rocking act that the term *lenggang perut* is derived. In this way, all the rest of the *sarong* are removed, and the last one thus taken out is given to the midwife together with the coconut, rice, *damar*, the *sireh*-box containing the money for services rendered and the token candles and yarn.

On the day of the *lenggang perut* ceremony, a small *kenduri* (quasi-religious ceremonial feast) is customarily held either immediately before or after the actual abdomen-rocking, and to this *kenduri* close relatives, neighbours and friends (mostly womenfolk), are invited, together with a couple of *lebai*. The pregnant wife is usually dressed in her best for the occasion.

2. THE ACTUAL DELIVERY OR CHILDBIRTH

When the nine months and nine days of the pregnancy are completed and the delivery of the child is expected any hour, all the materials —the same as those for the *lenggang perut* ceremony, but omitting the *sarong*—are made ready. There is also a difference in the payment for services rendered, which in this case is five dollars for the first-born child, three dollars and twenty-five cents for the second, and back again to five dollars for the third-born, while for the fourth and the rest, the payment is three dollars and twenty-five cents.

Before the child is delivered, it is even today customary among some of the rural Malays to hang a bunch of *mengkuang* leaves (pandanus thorny leaves) directly under that part of the house where the delivery will take place and where the mother will sleep during her taboo period. This is done because it is widely and superstitiously believed by the *kampong* Malays that there is a type of *hantu* (devil), that makes it its business to come during the delivery of a child, to enjoy drinking or eating the blood from childbirth, and who may do harm to both the mother and her newborn babe. The *mengkuang* leaves, they say, have the power to prevent the *hantu* or *shaitan* from coming close to the place of delivery, where the leaves are hung. It is also customary for a cross to be marked with a mixture of lime and water, at the door of the room where the mother and her newborn babe live during the taboo period. A cross is also made daily in the middle of the baby's forehead, between the eyebrows, with a mixture of oil and charcoal powder. Both these mixtures of lime and of charcoal are charmed with some spell or other by the *bidan* or a *bomo* (medicine-man) to frighten away the *hantu*. Although no longer practised by urban or educated Malays, as most of them have rid themselves of such beliefs or superstitions, this 'adat is still widely carried out among rural Malays.

## 3. Head-shaving and Naming of the Baby

Seven days after the delivery of the baby a ceremonial *kenduri* of *nasi kunyit* (yellow cooked rice) is held for the customary performance of shaving the head of the baby and naming him.

The preparations and the performance take place as follows:

(a) Invitations by letter or by word of mouth are sent to close relatives, neighbours and friends.

(b) The baby, prettily dressed, is laid on a tiny, beautifully embroidered mattress, placed on a silver or metal tray.

(c) Another tray is prepared with cups or saucers of yellow rice, parched rice (*berteh*) and a mixture of ground *setawar* leaves and water, called in Malay *ayer tepong tawar*.

(d) A very young coconut has its head or top part cut off in a zigzag pattern; the cut top serves as its lid or cover. The juice of the coconut is thrown away and replaced by pure water. This coconut is then decorated with artificial flowers made of silver, metal or plastic, and small silver or golden chains, and it is placed on a pedestalled tray.

(e) When all the guests have assembled, the baby is taken out to the male guests in the front hall.

(f) The ceremony then commences as the guests, one by one, throw first a little of the yellow rice around the baby, then the *berteh* (parched rice). Then they put a little of the *ayer tepong tawar* on the forehead of the baby, with a specially-made sprinkler of fragrant leaves. Each guest then takes the small pair of scissors that is provided for the purpose on the tray holding the baby, and cuts off a tiny lock of the baby's hair which he puts in the water inside the coconut. This performance is repeated by each of the guests, one after another. According to the *'adat* the number of those performing the ceremony should be odd, not even, for an even number is superstitiously believed to bring bad luck. After this, the baby and all the trays are taken inside to the female guests who repeat the performance of the ceremony. Only then is the baby given its name, usually chosen beforehand by the parents, after the usual consultation with the *'alim* (religious scholar), *bomo* (medicine-man) or the stars.

(g) After the guests have done their part, the *bidan* (or someone with better experience) performs the actual shaving of the head of the baby. All the shaved hair is put into the water in the young coconut; and after stripping it of all the decorations, it is planted somewhere in the compound of the house, and with it is also planted a young coconut palm or other tree to serve as a memorial of the baby's birth.

(h) Although this 'adat is not much practised by the town or modern Malays, it is still, to some extent, followed by the rural Malays. Malays are nowadays not very keen to have the tender head of a seven-day-old baby shaved, and this 'adat may soon either die out or be modified; but I think the quasi-religious feast on the completion of the seventh day after the baby's birth will probably survive among most of the rural Malays for many more years to come.

4. TEMPOH BERPANTANG (The Taboo Period)

For fully forty-four days to the hour from the day the baby is born, the mother is required by the 'adat to observe the usual *pantang* (taboo), which means that during that period she is not permitted to do as she likes, or to do even her usual domestic work. She has also to observe various food taboos — in fact she has to be on a very strict diet throughout the full forty-four days. For the first seven days the mother is not even allowed to leave the bed on which she gave birth to her baby. After the seventh day she may get up and walk about for short periods at a time, in the house only, but she is not to go out or go up and down the stairs in the house. This 'adat of *berpantang* was, in the olden days, very rigidly observed by all the Malays, without exception, and is still widely observed except by those who go to hospital for their delivery.

As to the medicine and treatment given to the mother in days gone by, nothing else would be accepted but the medicine and treatment of the *bidan* herself. The medicine was prepared from various herbs, for external or for internal use. The treatment was either *bertungku* (the application of a heated hearth stone to the abdomen of the mother for about a half to one hour once or twice daily) or *berdiang* (medicinal heating of the mother's abdomen and back alternately by charcoal fire, for about half an hour to one hour also once or twice daily). Although in the *kampong* a good many Malays still uphold and practise the old *'adat,* such traditional medicines and forms of treatment are not nearly as widely used now, since most of the enlightened Malays have learnt to take advantage of modern medicine and of treatment by qualified doctors and midwives. For this same reason the whole *'adat* of *berpantang* is also fast disappearing.

5. BATHING OF THE MOTHER TO END THE TABOO PERIOD

On the completion of the *pantang* (taboo) period of forty-four days from the day of delivery, it is customary, in accordance with the *'adat,* to perform the ceremonial bathing of the mother and to hold a small *kenduri*. A number of close relatives, neighbours and friends, mostly women, are invited, together with a couple of *lebai* (lower order of priests) or *'alim* to read the *do'a-selamat* (prayer of thanksgiving). The mother then undergoes the customary *mandi sintok limau* (ceremonial bath with *sintok* herbs and limes — *limau nipis* or *limau purut*, etc.), which is believed to be useful and effective for the dispelling of harm, danger and bad luck. Thus this ceremonial bath is also called in Malay *mandi tolak bala* (bath to dispel harm and misfortune). After these rites have been performed, the mother is released from the imprisonment of taboo, and can then do or eat whatever she likes without any fear of *betan* (recurrence of illness due to the violation of a taboo).

This, briefly, is the *'adat resam Melayu* for childbirth, which is still followed by quite a good number of Malays, especially those in the rural areas throughout the Malay Peninsula.

CHAPTER THREE

# MARRIAGE CUSTOMS

OF all the Malay *'adat resam* (customs and traditions), the *'adat resam kahwin* (marriage customs) are best liked and most adhered to by the majority of the Malays, urban as well as rural. They are prepared to go to any length, even to the extent of selling their property or borrowing money, for the purpose — and it requires quite a good deal of money to go through all the stages of the marriage ceremony in accordance with the *'adat*.

## A. MARRIAGE OF A MAIDEN

To facilitate a clear understanding of the *'adat* on marriage, I shall break my account up into three main stages and eight sub-stages, and explain each briefly:

*STAGE ONE* includes:

1. *Menilek* or *Menengok* (Investigation and selection of the bride-to-be)
2. *Meminang* or *Bertunang* (Engagement or betrothal)
3. *Menghantar Belanja dan 'Akad* (Sending of

dowry and expenses, and solemnisation of the marriage).

*STAGE TWO* includes:
1. *Berandam dan Berasah Gigi* (Hair-trimming and teeth-filing)
2. *Berhinai* (Staining the fingers and palms with henna).

*STAGE THREE* includes:
1. *Bersanding* (The sitting together of the groom and bride on the bridal couch)
2. *Mandi-mandi Berlimau* (Ceremonial bathing of the groom and bride after the third day of their marriage)
3. *Sambut-menyambut* (The escorting of the bride by the groom on her first visit to his house and then, after a couple of days, back to her own house).

I shall endeavour to explain each stage as briefly but as clearly as I can. But, at the outset, let me make one point in Stage One (1) clear — the *Menilek* or *Menengok* was, and still is, carried out in two different ways. One way is by consulting a fortune-teller, a *bomo*, a saintly person, or the stars. This was largely the way of Malays in bygone days, and, though not quite so much, the present-day rural Malays are still doing this, for a good number of them are superstitious. The other way is the more commonly adopted one, and it is of this that I shall write, for I personally believe it to be the right way.

## STAGE ONE

1. MENILEK OR MENENGOK
   (Selection and Study of the Bride-to-be)

As soon as the parents decide that their son has come to an age when he should marry, they start to look for a maiden suitable to be his wife. The responsibility of choosing the bride devolved entirely on the parents; but nowadays a good number of the enlightened Malays, particularly those with a Western education, leave the choice of a wife almost entirely to the sons themselves. There are also enlightened Malays who take the middle (and I should say the wisest) course, by which the parents choose the bride with the approval of their sons or vice versa. But notwithstanding all that, there are still a great number of die-hard Malays especially the rural ones, who adhere to the old 'adat, and they are undoubtedly in the majority.

The parents perform their task of selecting their son's bride seriously and thoroughly. After they have singled out a couple of maidens, they start their investigation machinery running, questioning friends and relatives, both their own and those of the maidens. The parents, in their investigations and their choice, require that not only the maiden but also her parents be of acceptable nature and character; for they, I think, hold fast to a Malay proverb which says, *"Kalau hendak meminang anak, 'pinang' ibu bapa-nya dahulu"*

("Before choosing a girl for marriage, choose the parents first").

The qualities most admired by prospective in-laws of olden days (and still by quite a good number of them even nowadays) were domestic abilities, such as cooking, sewing, and knitting. Over and above this, the attainment most highly admired was the ability of the maiden to read the Quran (not necessarily knowing the meaning of what she read) well and melodiously. No other scholastic attainment was, at that period, of any consideration at all, not even literacy in Malay.

Having gathered all the information they require, and having made their final choice of a daughter-in-law, and before making the formal application for her hand, the parents make their final examination by sending a couple of very intimate friends or relatives (usually women) to the house of the maiden to see her personally. Usually these messengers are sent without prior notice to the parents of the girl, for there is a significance in the impromptu visit, namely, it was traditionally believed by the Malays of olden times (and even by a few rural Malays today) that if, on their arrival, the messengers found the maiden in question bathing or washing, it was an omen of good luck for the future of the union of the two young persons. On the other hand if, on their arrival, they found the girl cooking in the kitchen, that was not such a good omen. It was also superstitiously believed that if, on their way to the girl's house, the messengers were delayed or prevented by any happening or accident, it portended a not-so-happy future for the marriage. Fortunately such superstitious beliefs have almost disappeared from among most of the Malays, even the rural ones.

At the end of the investigation and on being well satisfied with the results, the parents then call for a small get-together between their immediate family and close relatives, to decide on the best day for *meminang* (going to the maiden's parents to ask for the hand of their daughter in marriage).

2. MEMINANG AND BERTUNANG
   (Application for Bride's Hand and Betrothal)

The parents of the groom-to-be then select a couple of old people closely related to them, and depute them to approach the parents of the girl for their consent. Accordingly, the deputies carry out their mission to the letter; and it is customary (even though the parents of the girl have, prior to the arrival of the deputation, known of their coming, and have decided to give their consent), for the parents of the girl to ask for time to consider the application, with the excuse that they have to consult and obtain the approval of their kith and kin. This may take a couple of days or, at the most, a week. The parents of the girl then depute some of their relatives, both male and female this time, to deliver their message of acceptance; and it is there and then that the terms and conditions of the marriage, such as the dowry, expenses, etc. are discussed and settled, and the day for the marriage ceremony determined. This accounts for the inclusion of males in the deputation.

In the olden days, and also today to a lesser extent, the *'adat* of *Menghantar Tanda* (sending of a token) preceded the more important *'adat* of *Menghantar Maskahwin dan Belanja* (sending of dowry and expenses), especially if the solemnisation of the marriage was to be delayed for some months. The *tanda* (token) was usually in the form of a ring — either plain gold or diamond — the value of which depended entirely on the inclination and financial resources of the giver. It was also usual (and is so even today) for the *tanda* to be sent accompanied by presents for the bride-to-be, such as cloth, *sarong,* slippers or shoes, sweets, fruits, etc.

The sending of the *tanda* (engagement ring) is customarily accompanied by ceremonial *kenduri* held by both sides. Some even take the ring and other presents in procession to the house of the bride-to-be. The acceptance of the engagement ring and the presents, in accordance with the *'adat,* means also the acceptance of customary terms and conditions binding to both parties.
They are:
(a) If, for any reason whatsoever, the man should fail to marry the girl to whom he is thus betrothed, the engagement ring, together

with the rest of the presents given to the girl, cannot be claimed back.

(b) Should the girl, for any reason except her own death, fail to fulfil the objects and aims of the betrothal, then the *tanda,* together with all the other articles presented, should be returned to the man, doubled either in number or in value. Such has been the ʻ*adat* followed by the Malays for generations.

NOTE

Two ways of *bertunang* (engagement), other than the above mentioned, have also been accepted and are practised by the Malays. They are:

(i) Engagement for marriage made by two very intimately friendly or related families between their son and daughter while they are still infants or children, without any engagement ring or written agreement, is a tradition widely respected and adhered to, and happy marriages have often followed such engagements.

(ii) Engagement or betrothal, made in fulfilment of the wish (either verbally expressed before death or written in the will) of a deceased parent is also very highly honoured by the Malays, and very often marriages which result from such engagements turn out to be happy ones.

3. MENGHANTAR BELANJA AND ʻAKAD
   (Sending of Dowry and Solemnisation of Marriage)

In olden days the ceremony of sending the dowry and expenses of marriage took place a day or two (sometimes even more) before the *'akad* (solemnisation of the marriage), but nowadays both the ceremonies are usually held on the same day with a view, I think, to economy.

NOTE

(i) It is not unusual that the *maskahwin* (dowry) agreed upon is not sent or paid in cash, but remains on credit, *berhutang;* in either case it will be declared by the *kadhi* (the religious official who solemnises the marriage.

(ii) The amount for the dowry may be given to the bridegroom who will himself hand it over to the *kadhi* at the marriage ceremony.

Apart from the dowry and money for expenses agreed upon, the following are the items sent:

(i) A ring set with a precious stone
(ii) Silk, sufficient for one lady's *baju* (coat)
(iii) Two *sarong,* also of silk
(iv) An assortment of home-made cakes
(v) An assortment of fruits
(vi) A *puan* (betel-bowl) or *sireh*-box complete with its ingredients (this is not included as a present)
(vii) One or two rose-water sprinklers of silver or of brass — also to be returned.

All the above articles accompany the bridegroom in the procession to the bride's house, where the marriage is solemnised. On this occasion of *'akad,* the bridegroom, in the olden days, usually wore either *haji* dress (a long robe and a turban) or the simple Malay national costume. The wearing of the costume at that time was, to the people's conservative belief, a token of respect to the solemnisation of the marriage. The *'akad* is, in fact the one and only ceremony that is essentially required by Islam and the law of the country to make the marriage *halal* (sanctioned). All the other marriage rites are only the requirements of the *'adat resam*.

On arrival at the bride's house, the procession is received and led in. The bridegroom is seated on a *tikar-sila* (square ceremonial mat) in the main part of the hall, close to the *kadhi*, and the articles he brought are put in a line in the middle of the hall, between the two lines of seated guests, with the expense-money, the ring and the *puan* at the head of the line.

The *kadhi* then selects two from among the guests to be witnesses, to receive and check the *hantaran* (things sent) as well as to witness the solemnisation of the marriage.

After all the articles, starting with the expense-money and ring, have been checked and formally accepted by the *kadhi* on behalf of the parents of the bride, they are sent inside to the women. All, that is, except the *puan*, the rose-water sprinklers and, if provided, the tray of *bunga rampai* (fragrantly-scented leaves and flowers). Then the *kadhi* registers the name of the bridegroom in a book, and after the entry has been signed by the bridegroom and counter-signed by the said two witnesses, the kadhi reads the marriage service in Arabic, as of old. (Nowadays, however, quite a good number of Malay *kadhi* very sensibly read the service in the language understood by the groom and all the guests present.) At the end of the service, the *kadhi* takes hold of the groom's right hand, and pronounces the statement of the *'akad* to the groom, first in Arabic (this is optional), then in Malay: "*Hey...bin...., aku nikah-kan dikau dengan... binti...yang telah memperwakili ia akan daku dengan maskahwin-nya sabanyak* $... (*tunai/berhutang*) *dan belanja-nya* $..." — "Lo...son of ..., I bestow to you in marriage...daughter of... who has made me his representative (and on whose behalf) I accept your dowry of $...(rendered/promised) together with your contribution (towards wedding expenses) of $...." He then shakes the groom's hand as a sign for him to answer, without flaw or hesitation: "*Aku terima nikah-nya...binti..., dengan maskahwin-nya* $... (*tunai/berhutang*) *dan belanja-nya* $..." —"With this dowry of $...(rendered/promised) and this contribution (towards marriage expenses) of $..., I receive in marriage...daughter of...."

NOTE

Custom allows that the *maskahwin* be paid, not in cash, but on credit, with no mention of the date of its payment. Thus the *kadhi* will add the word *berhutang* (on credit) or *tunai* (cash) immediately after saying the amount of the *maskahwin* in his statement in the *'akad*.

If the answer comes unhesitatingly and clearly and can be heard by those sitting near the groom, particularly by the said two witnesses, then the marriage is taken to be duly and legally solemnised. (In days gone by, the consent of the bride was presumed if she were a maiden, but was officially obtained by the *kadhi* if she were a widow. In any case this, among other particulars required for registration were settled before the arrival of the bridegroom.) After the *'akad,* the bridegroom shakes hands with all the guests present, starting with the *kadhi* and father of the bride, should he be present in the gathering. Then the groom is escorted back to his house and the guests, both male and female, in the bride's house, are entertained with the customary *jamuan* (feast) of curry and rice enriched with oil.

At the same time it is customary for the bride's party to prepare the ceremonial *nasi pengantin* (complete dinner specially prepared for the bridegroom), and to send it to him at his house, where it is also customary for the bridegroom to invite a few of his most intimate friends to feast with him.

## STAGE TWO

In accordance with prior agreement between the two parties, the third stage of the marriage ceremony, which is the *bersanding* (the sitting together of the groom and the bride on the *pelamin* — bridal-couch) is held usually on the same evening of, or on the day after, the *'akad* ceremony; but it is not unusual for the *bersanding* to be carried out some days after the *'akad,* although it is seldom more than two or three days later. In the latter case, it is during these three days that the second stage, *berandam* and the three ceremonies of *berhinai* (henna-staining) — namely *berhinai-churi,* (private henna-staining), *berhinai-kechil* (semi-public henna-staining), and *berhinai-besar* (public henna-staining) — are held at the bride's house.

1. BERANDAM AND BERASAH GIGI
   (Hair-trimming and Teeth-filing)

This customary practice of trimming the hair and filing the teeth of the bride was widely carried out by Malays in the past, but the practice has almost died out nowadays. The custom, with its accompanying ceremony, was usually observed about three or more days before the day fixed for the *'akad.* The bride's hair along her forehead, and her eyebrows as well, were neatly trimmed (quite often, even the bridegroom had to undergo this ceremonial grooming). Then the bride's teeth were filed and polished to make them look even and glossy. This work was done by the *tukang andam* (skilled hair-trimmer) who was also the *emak pengantin* (lady chosen to act as "bride-mother" throughout the marriage ceremony, as is still the custom today). But, nowadays, it is only the *berandam* that is still performed on the bride (no longer on the groom) by the *kampong* Malays, while the town or modern

Malays prefer to send their brides-to-be to the present-day beauty-parlours that abound in all towns in Malaya. But in remote places, there are those who still keep to the '*adat,* in blind obedience to the Malay proverb, which says: "*Biar mati anak, jangan mati 'adat*". "The death of one's own child is preferable to the lapse of an '*adat.*")

After the trimming of the hair, the bride is ceremonially bathed with *ayer sintok-limau* (water which contains limes and the bark of the *sintok* tree), which is traditionally believed to have the power of ridding the girl of harm and misfortune.

After the ceremonial bath and on the same evening before she sleeps, the tips of all ten fingers, the centre of the palms of both her hands, and all the edges of the soles of her feet are stained with henna, and left untouched till dry the next morning. This is the real henna-staining, and it precedes the so-called *berhinai* ceremonies.

2. BERHINAI CEREMONIES (Henna-staining)

The first of these other ceremonial practices is called *berhinai churi* (private henna-staining). This is held on the evening of the day after the girl's fingers, palms and soles have been stained. The girl is adorned, and seated on the *pelamin* and the same procedure is carried out as will be explained later for the ceremony of *berhinai besar* (the third and final henna-staining ceremony). On the evening after the *berhinai churi,* comes the second ceremony, the *berhinai kechil,* following the same procedure.

At the *berhinai besar* (public henna-staining) both the bridegroom and the bride ascend the *pelamin* on the same evening, but one after the other. The procedure is as follows:

(a) When the bridegroom, dressed in wedding garments, arrives at the bride's house, he is led in and seated on the *pelamin* before a gathering of invited guests (mostly women), close relatives, neighbours and friends of the bride's family.

(b) Before the groom on the *pelamin* is placed one large pedestalled tray, holding three plates or saucers — one containing yellow rice; another, *berteh* (parched rice); and the third, a mixture of ground *setawar* leaves and water, together with its sprinkler, specially made from sweet-scented leaves. In the centre of the tray, is placed a neatly-shaped mound of henna paste.

(c) The ceremony commences with the male guests coming up, one by one, to the groom on the *pelamin,* taking first a little of the yellow rice, and throwing some to the right, and some to the left, of the groom. Then the same is done with the parched rice or *berteh.* Next the guest takes the sprinkler of leaves and dips it lightly in the mixture of *setawar* leaves, and touches the backs of both the groom's hands with it. Lastly, he takes a pinch of the henna paste from the mound at the centre of the tray and puts it on the *sireh* leaf previously placed by the *emak pengantin* on the upturned palms of the groom's hands, to prevent them from being stained. Immediately after that the *emak pengantin* takes both hands of the groom, puts the palms and fingers together and raises them up to about the chest level as a sign of *menyembah* (paying respect) to the guest performing the ceremony. This ceremony is customarily performed by all the guests who so desire, but the number, according to the *'adat*, should be odd, not even.

(d) When the male guests have finished, the women guests take their turn, performing the ceremony in exactly the same manner. After that, a man of religion from among the male guests comes forward and reads the blessing, *do'a selamat*.

(e) After the bridegroom has left for his own house, the bride, in her turn, is led out and seated on the *pelamin* to undergo the same ceremony.

(f) The ceremony is closed, as usual, with a *jamuan* of curry and rice. The *kenduri* or feasts during the *berhinai churi* and *berhinai kechil* are very small compared with the *kenduri* at the *berhinai besar* ceremony. Besides, at the *berhinai churi* and *berhinai kechil* the bride alone undergoes the ceremony, in her house. As for the bridegroom, some Malays in the olden days may have performed the henna ceremony on him in his house as well, but this is no longer done.

## STAGE THREE

1. BERSANDING (The Sitting Together of the Bridegroom and Bride on the Bridal Couch)

Before recounting the different stages in '*adat bersanding*, I shall try to describe briefly the *pelamin* (bridal-couch) and its preparation.

The form of the *pelamin* is roughly similar to that of the *Singgahsana* (throne) of a Malay *raja* of olden days, with its *peterakna* (dais) made of wood and cardboard, beautifully decorated and covered with gleaming silk or paper of various colours, and decorated also with small colourful lights (formerly of coconut-oil lamps, and nowadays of coloured electric bulbs). The size and grandeur of the *pelamin* depends entirely on the financial means and the status of the bride's family. The height of the *pelamin* (its platform only) is usually not more than three tiers, each about a foot high. The *peterakna* (dais) on which the bridal pair sits surmounts the *pelamin*, and is covered with silk or velvet, beautifully embroidered. In front of the dais, and on the topmost tier of the *pelamin*, is placed an *astakona* (an octagonal shaped pedestalled tray) containing a well-moulded mound of cooked yellow rice, studded all over with *bunga-telor merah* (eggs painted or dyed red, impaled on sticks of bamboo which are topped with artificial flowers). At the summit of the mound of yellow rice is placed a big *tajok* (bouquet) of artificial flowers, made from *kertas perada* (tinsel or gold or silver foil) and other flower-papers.

When everything else is ready for the *bersanding* ceremony (which usually takes place in the evening, after the feasting) and the bride's attendants begin to dress her, a messenger is immediately sent to the bridegroom's house to inform him and his party of the approximate hour at which they are expected to arrive at the bride's house for the ceremony. A second and last message is sent when the bride is almost completely dressed. In this way she can avoid having to wait, and to suffer unnecessarily from the weight of her head-dress and costume, which are usually much heavier than any other type of Malay ceremonial dress.

After the bride has donned the Malay bridal dress, complete with head-gear, made from silver, gold and precious stones, she is led out of her room by the *emak pengantin*. She walks very slowly, with eyes almost closed, and a little girl, her *pengapit* (bridesmaid), also beautifully dressed, walks by her side. The bride is then seated on the left side of the *peterakna* (dais) of the *pelamin* and the girl *pengapit*, standing on her left, fans her slowly with a beautifully embroidered fan. Throughout the period that she is on the *pelamin*, in accordance with the *'adat*, the bride must sit with head bowed and eyes almost closed, as a token of modesty and shyness, which in the olden days were looked upon as the highest of womanly qualities.

At the same time that the bride is led from her room to the *pelamin*, the groom is also escorted from his house on the usual wedding procession to the bride's house. But if the bride's house is far away, or if it is intended that the procession should take a longer time to go through the town or village, then the groom leaves some time before the bride emerges from her room. The bridegroom usually wears full Malay dress, complete with *destar* or *tengkolok* (head-dress), *bengkong* (waistband) and *keris*. In the olden days it was customary for the bridegroom to be carried on the shoulders of his attendants or in a hammock-litter, or to ride in a carriage. But nowadays he goes by car.

Leading the procession are groups of young men beating the *rebana* or the *kompang* (two types of timbrels), sometimes both, and reading in rhythm Arabic verses praising the Prophet Muhammad. Immediately behind these groups there is usually an elderly man, carrying a *puan* (betel-bowl or *sireh*-box) complete with its ingredients. The *puan* is covered with a specially-made cover of silver or metal in the shape of a peacock's head. On each side of the *puan*-bearer walks a young man carrying a lighted candle in a candlestick. Behind the *puan*- and candlestick-bearers the bridegroom walks, or is carried in an *usongan* (hammock-litter). A boy, dressed in Malay costume, as resplendent as the bridegroom himself, sits in the litter beside the bridegroom. One or two older men (representing the groom's parents), either accompany them in the litter, or walk in the procession. Behind them walk all the rest of the groom's relatives and friends — the groom's father and mother are not usually there. The procession used to be lighted by hand-made torches of coconut oil (*andang*) carried by men walking on each side of the procession. All along the journey the groups of *rebana* and *kompang* singers (and nowadays orchestral parties) and other musical groups perform their music. A group of ladies from the bridegroom's family is sent ahead to the bride's house, as an advance-guard to announce the coming of the bridegroom. They are received by the ladies of the bride, who first sprinkle yellow rice and rose-water over the newcomers' heads and then take them to a place specially reserved for them, in front of the *pelamin*.

In the open space or compound of the bride's house a crowd of people gather to welcome the bridegroom. In this crowd too there are *rebana* or *kompang* parties and other musical parties, standing in the same order as those in the groom's procession, waiting to welcome the arrival of the procession. In front of the crowd is a man bearing a *puan* with its cover of silver or metal in the form of the head of a peahen. A candle-stick-bearer stands on each side. The *rebana* and *kompang* singers, on seeing the procession approaching, immediately start beating the timbrels and singing in praise of the Prophet Muhammad.

When the procession arrives it stops at a place about ten to twenty yards away from the bride's house, and faces the bride's party. Then the *puan*-carrier of the groom makes a sign challenging the *puan*-carrier of the bride to come forward to receive him. The answer is a counter-challenge for the groom's *puan*-carrier to come first. This challenge is immediately accepted, and here commences the *tarian silat* (self-defence dance) between the two *puan*-carriers, with the crowd cheering and clapping their hands to show their appreciation and admiration. The *puan*-carriers stop immediately they come close enough for the heads of the peacock and peahen covers of the *puan* to touch each other, and this receives the final and loudest cheers from the crowd. (At one time the Malays were very particular about the selection of the *puan*-carriers, for they valued this *'adat* very highly, and so they usually selected the best dancers available in the *kampong*.) The bridegroom is then taken to the front door of the house, where a melodious-voiced young man reads loudly three times the verses blessing the Prophet, to ensure the safe and blessed entry of the groom into the house. It was and still is usual to spread a narrow carpet or piece of cloth from about a couple of yards in front of the front door right up to the front edge of the *pelamin*, for the bridegroom to walk on.

Before the groom could be escorted through the front door into the house it was an observed *'adat* that the bridegroom's party be made to pay what they called *tebus pintu* (door tax). This was enforced by posting a few youths — sitting or standing — in line in front of the door, to bar the bridegroom from going in before a token payment of a few dollars had been paid to the leader of the group. If, with luck, there was only one door to pass through before reaching the *pelamin*, then there would be no more door tax to be paid by the groom. But at the lowest tier of the *pelamin* was another group, this time of young ladies, sitting down to bar the groom from ascending the *pelamin* before paying another tax, called *tebus pelamin* (bridal-couch tax), which might be higher than the door tax. The last and the highest tax to be paid was what they called *tebus kipas* (fan tax). It was enforced when the groom was already up on the *pelamin* and facing the bride, whose face was screened with a fan by the *emak pengantin*. This fan would not be taken away from the front of the bride's face, and the groom would not be allowed to see her face or to sit beside his bride until the tax was paid to the *emak pengantin*. This was the highest tax of all. (This taxing is no longer practised nowadays as an '*adat*, but some Malays may adopt it just for fun.)

The bridegroom is then made to sit on the right of the bride, on the dais, and his *pengapit* (the boy who acts as his best man) stands beside him on the right, fanning him slowly. The bridegroom and his bride resemble a *Sultan* and his *Sultana* on their thrones, receiving the homage of their people. Thus the term *Raja sa-hari* (King for a day) came to be used when referring to the bridegroom. The guests, now packed in the hall before the *pelamin*, are all women and young children, for, truth to tell, this *bersanding* ceremony has ever been and ever will be an affair of the womenfolk, for the majority of Malay women, even most of the modern women, will not consider any marriage ceremony complete and proper without it.

While both the groom and bride are on the *pelamin* feasting the eyes of the womenfolk before them, the '*adat bersuap-suapan* (ceremonial and mutual feeding of yellow rice between the bridal pair) is supervised by the *emak pengantin*. She takes a pinch of the yellow rice from the decorated mound which stands in the *astakona* (the octagonal-shaped pedestalled tray) and, putting it between two fingers of the bride's right hand, lifts it to the lips of the bridegroom as a symbol of being fed by the bride herself. In like manner the bridegroom feeds the bride. As soon as the '*adat bersuap-suapan* is over, the *emak pengantin* leaves the pair and comes down to call the male guests (who have not seen the *bersanding* as yet) to come up, in separate groups, for just a few seconds. After all have seen the *bersanding*, the *emak pengantin* escorts both the groom and his bride down from the *pelamin*. The groom links the little finger of his left hand to that of his wife's right hand, and they are slowly led to their beautifully prepared and decorated bridal chamber, where they are seated on two *tikar-sila* (ceremonial mats) before the decorated bridal bed. The *emak pengantin* then guides the bride's hands in a ceremonial hand-clasp with the bridegroom. This represents their first introduction to each other. They are then left alone for an hour or two, so that they may get to know each other. "Love after marriage" was the rule with the olden-day Malays, and still holds good today. Although quite a good number of the more modern Malays do not take this rule as seriously as their fathers and grandfathers did, there are still greater numbers, in both the rural and urban areas, among both the educated and uneducated, who do not favour the idea of love before marriage.

After an hour or two, the *emak pengantin* returns to lead the bride away to a separate chamber. The groom is left to sleep alone in the bridal chamber, not on the bridal dais or bedstead, but on special bedding prepared for him. It is customary that the bridal dais or bedstead remain unused until the evening that the groom and the bride first sleep together — that is, on the third or fourth evening after the *bersanding*. The next morning, after the bride is dressed in her best attire, she is sent into the bridal chamber with a tray of breakfast which she shares with her husband. She is left with her husband in the room until some time before lunch, when she leaves for another change of attire. She returns to have lunch with him, and is again allowed to stay with him till tea time. She is then led away for yet another change of dress, and returns to dine with her husband. They are then left alone together, but she later takes her leave to sleep in a separate room by herself. The same procedure is adopted throughout three whole days and nights.

But on the evening of the third day or, in some cases, of the fourth, the bridal dais is prepared for both the groom and his bride to sleep together for the first time since their marriage. The bed-sheets and pillow-cases are changed from ceremonial and colourful ones to new white ones. After dinner the bride is led away to be dressed in the special white costume customarily worn by a Malay bride during her first night with her husband. During the first half of the night it used to be the custom to hold some sort of light musical entertainment, such as *zapin* (a mixture of Arab and Malay music and dancing), or some other form of entertainment available in the area, for the delight of the new couple.

2. MANDI-MANDI BERLIMAU (Ceremonial Bathing after Marriage)

Before the bathing ceremony is performed, another important tradition is observed. This last was widely practised in days gone by and is still followed today, though to a lesser extent and chiefly in the *kampong*. Early in the morning, after the night of consummation, the *emak pengantin* asks the bridegroom for concrete proof of the bride's virginity. The bridegroom customarily hands over a white handkerchief which bears the required evidence. The *emak pengatin* then shows the handkerchief, first to the parents of the bride, and then, most important of all, to the parents of the bridegroom. In olden days, proof of the bride's virginity was of utmost importance to Muslims generally. It was compulsory to furnish the evidence before the *mandi-mandi* ceremony could be performed. It was so important that its absence almost always gave rise to great trouble that often resulted in an immediate divorce. Although the *'adat* is less widely observed today, there are still a good number of Malays who insist on the practice.

After both the groom's and the bride's parents have been fully satisfied as to the purity or "honour" of the bride, the *mandi-mandi* ceremony can take place. The husband and wife are again dressed in their best attire and seated again on the *pelamin* before a group of guests from among the relatives, neighbours and close friends of both the families of the groom and the bride. This time they are dressed not in bridal attire but in ordinary Malay national costume. After sitting thus for ten to fifteen minutes, they are led down and seated on a bench or two chairs in a hall or room in the house, where the token ceremonial bath is carried out by the *emak pengantin*. It consists of sprinkling both the groom and the bride with water of *sintok* (bark of a tree, used for cleaning hair) and *limau purut* (medicinal lemon). After the ceremony has been completed, the groom leads the bride back to the bridal chamber, each holding on to one end of a handkerchief. The *sarong* used by both the husband and wife in the ceremony are given away to the *emak pengantin*, not only as gifts, but as *tolak bala* and *buang geroh* (repelling misfortune and harm). Neither bride nor groom is allowed even to squeeze out the water from either of the *sarong*, let alone keep or wear it again. That was the *'adat* that used to be observed and adhered to, but these days the whole *mandi-mandi* ceremony is being discarded by most Malays, particularly those in the urban areas, though in the rural areas it is still practised by the die-hards.

3. SAMBUT-MENYAMBUT (The Bride's First Visit to the Groom's Home and Her Return to Her Own Home)

On the day of the bathing ceremony a *kenduri* is held in the bride's house. Meanwhile her husband and his parents take her on her first visit to their house. Here the newly-weds again undergo the *bersanding* ceremony if the parents are well-to-do people. There another feast or *kenduri* is held, to which some hundreds of men and women are invited. Sometimes day and night entertainment of local music and dancing, such as either *joget* or *ma'yong* or both are held to entertain the bride. Not infrequently the ceremony held in the house of the groom on the occasion of the *menyambut* is on a scale equal to, or sometimes greater than the first *bersanding* ceremony at the bride's house. After remaining for a few days in her husband's house, the wife, accompanied by her husband and her own parents, returns to her house, where the couple will live, at least for a few months. On this occasion too there is the usual *kenduri* (feast) but it is a comparatively small one.

NOTE

The quasi-religious feasts, or *kenduri*, can be said to be carried out in almost the same manner all over the Malay

Peninsula, except for some differences of system and time between those held in the northern and those in the southern states. In almost all the three main stages and in most of the sub-stages mentioned above, *kenduri* are held, and the biggest of them all take place during the *'akad* and the *bersanding* ceremonies, in the house of both the bride and the bridegroom; but it is usual that the wedding *kenduri* at the bride's house are more numerous and grander than those held in the bridegroom's house.

Thus, briefly, have been described the three stages of the marriage ceremony, as performed in accordance with *'adat resam Melayu*.

## B. MARRIAGE OF A WIDOW

It is ruled by Islam that a widow (*bujang* or *janda* in Malay), or a woman whose marriage has been terminated or annulled, can only be legally married again after a period of three months and ten days from the day of her husband's decease, her divorce, or from the day after the dissolution or annulment (*pasah*) of her marriage by judicial decree. This period of three months and ten days is termed *edah*. Malay widows, particularly those in the *kampong* (who for the most part are ill-educated), almost entirely depend, when looking for another husband, on their good looks, behaviour and domestic ability and of course in some cases, wealth. In fact it can safely be said that a *janda kaya* (wealthy widow) can get married again more easily and more quickly than a less wealthy woman in the same situation, and this is as true in the *kampong* as it is in the town.

The following is the customary procedure for the marriage of widows:

1. MEMINANG JANDA (To Ask for the Hand of a Widow in Marriage)

The requirements of '*adat* in this case are very much simpler, and the marriage ceremony can be accomplished within a day or even a few hours. The man who has decided to ask a widow to be his wife may not care to know more than a few facts about her present condition, personality, and circumstances.

He or his parents then send an old, respectable lady to the widow's house to see the widow's parents, if they are still living, and then the widow herself, who in this case is entitled by the '*adat* to have her own say in the acceptance or rejection of the application of marriage. But even today, as of old, among many Malays both in the urban and rural areas, if the widow happens to be still very young and beautiful and has no issue from her former husband, she is considered by her parents, to be as good (or almost as good) as a maiden, and all the requirements of the '*adat* for the marriage of a maiden are followed. Such a marriage is termed in Malay:

2. PERKAHWINAN JANDA BERHIAS (Marriage Ceremony for a Young Childless Widow)

The young widow and the groom go through almost all the procedures of the marriage ceremony, as though she were an *anak dara* (maiden), including the *bersanding*, but not the *mandi-mandi* (ceremonial bath after the third day of marriage). Otherwise the marriage of a widow only requires the *ʻakad* (solemnisation of the marriage), and one *kenduri* for *doʻa selamat* immediately after the *ʻakad*.

CHAPTER FOUR

# FUNERAL CUSTOMS

1. It has been observed as an *'adat resam* for generations that when a death occurs in a family in either *kampong* or town, the first step to be taken by the family of the deceased is to inform the *siak* (caretaker) of the mosque in the vicinity, so that the name of the deceased, the time of death, and the time and place of burial, can be posted on the notice-board of the mosque for the general information of the people in the community. Moreover, the *siak* is informed (either the same day or the next) so that he can have the grave dug and prepared in time for the burial, as the place of interment is usually in the burial ground of the same mosque. After the *siak,* all close relatives and friends of the family are informed.

2. If the death occurs in the afternoon or evening, the funeral is usually fixed for some time in the afternoon, or at the latest in the evening, of the next day. But if the death occurs in the early morning, the funeral will be held the same afternoon or evening, for the Muslim religion requires

that the dead be interred as soon as possible. Islam in fact enjoins that the burial of a dead body should not be unnecessarily delayed for more than six hours after death.

3. First, the body of the deceased is placed on either a dais or bedstead with mattress and clean sheets. The dais is usually placed in the main hall of the house, within easy approach of relatives and friends who come to have a last look at the deceased. Above the dais or bedstead, a ceiling of cloth is strung to prevent dust or particles of attap from falling on the dead body, but such a precaution is no longer necessary in more up-to-date houses. The *mayat* (dead body) is laid on its back, with both hands folded on the chest, and is covered from head to foot with a couple of silk sheets. In the middle of the body, between the chest and abdomen, outside the top sheet is placed a *kachip* (areca-nut slicer) in the customary belief that it serves as a *tangkal* (talisman) to keep away ghosts or *shaitan* (spirits of evil) and prevent them from jumping or passing over the *mayat*. Close in front of the dais is an incense-burner, with *setanggi* (home-made incense) or *gaharu* (agila-wood) burning throughout the period the *mayat* is in the house, and sometimes until three days after the funeral.

4. While the materials for use in the bathing of the *mayat*, and the cloth for the *kapan* (shroud), and the coffin are being prepared, the relatives and close friends of the deceased are invited, if they

wish, to come and take their last look at the deceased. They come, one after another, very quietly and respectfully, lift the covering, look at the face for an instant, then go out.

5. It is required by Malay *'adat* that as long as the *mayat* is in the house, all the visitors, male or female without any exception whatsoever, as well as the neighbours living close by, must show respect to the dead by not making any noise or speaking loudly or disrespectfully. This is required not only by the Malay *'adat* but also enjoined by Islam. In the same manner also, respect should be shown throughout the whole of the funeral — from the time that the procession leaves the house. The members of this procession should not engage in conversation. Instead, they should read the opening chapter of the Quran slowly all along the journey to the graveyard, as a last good deed for the deceased.

6. When it is time for the *mayat* to be bathed, the body is carried by male relatives if the deceased is male, or by female relatives if the deceased is female, to the place for the quasi-religious bath. This is performed by the *tukang mandi mayat* (a woman if the deceased is female, and a man if the deceased is male), who carries out his duties carefully and thoroughly, and in a respectful manner. After the bathing, the whole body of the *mayat* is smeared with two types of powder, namely, camphor and yellow sandalwood;

and the powder is especially smeared under the armpits and on all the joints of the limbs. Lastly, pieces of cotton wool are placed at the necessary parts of the body. The body is then carried to the hall or front portion of the house, where it is to be shrouded (*kapankan*). The wrapping sheet, among the Malays and other Muslims, is made into a tunic and trousers for the body but they must NOT be stitched or sewn. After the tunic and trousers have been put on the body, it is further wrapped up in a shroud of white cloth which is also unstitched and unsewn. These two sets of grave-clothes for the *mayat* comprise what the Malay call *kapan mayat*. After the body has been wrapped with the outer sheet, it is tied with tape-like twines, made from the same cloth, from the feet up to the neck at intervals of about a foot or so, leaving the head end still untied; for before the head is wrapped up and tied, the relatives who wish, are customarily called to sprinkle some sandalwood powder around it as a last service rendered to the deceased. After this, the head is wrapped up and tied, and the body is then put in the coffin. This is made of light wood, and has no bottom. Instead, a piece of white cloth is stretched underneath to close the opening. This complies with the requirement of Islam that the body should rest directly on the earth or ground. After putting the lid on the coffin, it is draped with a few sheets of silk or other materials, finely woven, and the topmost sheet usually has verses from the

Quran written or embroidered all over it. On the top of this fresh flowers are sometimes scattered. The coffin is put on a litter and carried to the mosque adjoining the graveyard, or, if there is none, to any mosque close by or on the way to the graveyard, where the *mayat* is given a congregational prayer before interment. This is only done if prayers have not already been said in the house. It is customary that those who pray for the *mayat* in the congregation are each given a token gift of money, from twenty to fifty cents, or even a dollar, if the deceased was a very wealthy person.

7. From the mosque to the grave the coffin is carried by a few men, mostly relatives and friends of the deceased. The *siak* (caretaker of the mosque) and the grave-digger together with one of the relatives or friends who wishes to perform his last service for the deceased, wait in the grave to receive the lowered coffin. The *siak* then removes the lid, unties all the cloth tapes tying the body from head to foot, and turns the body on to its right side, facing towards the *Qiblat* (i.e. Mecca). The *siak* then puts balls of earth, made by relatives and friends from the excavated earth of the grave, between the body and the two walls of the coffin, to keep the body firmly in place. Finally the *siak* calls into the ear of the *mayat* the usual call to prayer, and then closes the coffin with its lid or cover, and he and his helpers leave the grave to allow a couple of men to start filling it in. When this is done, a small branch of

a tree in the graveyard is plucked and planted on the grave, at the spot where the head of the body lies, just to mark the position where the tomb-stone is to be placed later. But there are also cases when the tomb-stones are placed on the graves at the same time as the interment.

8. As soon as the filling in of the grave is completed, an *Imam*, usually the *Imam* of the mosque nearest to the graveyard, or someone who is noted as a religious teacher and friend of the deceased, or a *kadhi*, comes forward close to the grave, by the side of which is a square mat or *tikar-sila* wrapped with silk cloth or *sarong*. On this is found a tray of *bunga rampai* (fragrant leaves cut into very minute shreds, mixed with some flowers and sprinkled with rose-water or perfume) and one or two glass containers or jugs of sandalwood water. The *Imam* sits on the mat and starts reading or reciting from memory, in Arabic, the *Talqin* (exhortation to the dead). In some cases, if the deceased was a very wealthy person, the *Imam* is sheltered by a fine umbrella of cloth or paper while he reads, even though there be no rain or sunshine falling on him. (This was customary at one time but is no longer common.) After reading the *Talqin*, he leads the assembled people in the *Tahlil* (praising God by repeating the first word of the Creed—"*la ilaha ila Allah*"); and then the *do'a selamat* (prayer for blessing). After this the sandalwood water is poured over the grave, from head to foot, and

then the flowers on the tray are scattered all over the grave.  The reader of the *Talqin*, besides being paid two to five dollars or more, is also presented with the mat he sat on when reading the *Talqin*, the empty glass containers which held sandalwood water and also with the umbrella that sheltered him during his recitation of the *Talqin*.

9. It must have been since the time that the Malays were first converted to Islam that they have been taught, and have consequently adopted the practice (one of their most important *'adat*) to hold quasi-religious ceremonies, which they call *kenduri arwah* (feast for the soul of the dead). The object of these feasts is that the soul of the dead man may receive the blessing of God in the hereafter. This 'adat is upheld by Malays to this day, but the truth is that Islam NEVER enjoins any *kenduri* whatsoever to help the dead in the hereafter.

# PART TWO

## ROYAL MALAY CUSTOMS & TRADITIONS

'ADAT ISTI'ADAT DIRAJA MELAYU

CHAPTER ONE

# LANGUAGE, ETIQUETTE AND ANCIENT LAWS

## A. 'ADAT ISTI'ADAT BAHASA TERHADAP RAJA
(LANGUAGE TRADITIONALLY USED FOR ROYALTY)

The following words are used only when speaking to or of persons of royal descent:

(i) *TITAH* — (SAY) — to the reigning *raja* (*Sultan*) and his consort (*Sultana*) only

(ii) *SABDA* — (SAY) — to all *anak2 raja* only (princes and princesses)

\* (iii) *PATEK* — (I or ME) — used only when speaking to a *Sultan, Sultana* or *Raja Perempuan* (reigning queen) and to all *anak2 raja* in almost all Malay countries

---

\* Nowadays in Johore and Trengganu PATEK is only used when speaking to the reigning monarch and his descendants, while for the rest of *anak2 raja* HAMBA-TENGKU or HAMBA-ENGKU is used. But in all the rest of the Malay States PATEK is used when speaking to both the reigning monarch and all *anak2 raja* as well.

(iv) *MURKA* — (ANGRY) — originally to the reigning monarch only, but now to all of royal blood

(v) *KURNIA* — (GIVE or GRANT) — to the reigning monarch and to all *anak2 raja*

(vi) *ANUGERAH* — (GIVE or ENDOW) — to the reigning monarch and all *anak2 raja*

(vii) *SANTAP* — (EAT or DRINK) — to the reigning monarch and all *anak2 raja*

\* (viii) *SILA* — (COME or INVITE to) — to the reigning monarch and all *anak2 raja*

(ix) *BERADU* — (SLEEP) — to the reigning monarch as well as to *anak2 raja*

(x) *GERING* — (ILL or SICK) — to the reigning monarch and all *anak2 raja*

(xi) *MANGKAT* — (DIE) — to the reigning monarch and all *anak2 raja*

(xii) *SEMAYAM* — (SIT) — to the reigning monarch and all *anak2 raja*

(xiii) *BERSIRAM* — (BATHE) — to the reigning monarch and all *anak2 raja*

(xiv) *PACHAL* — (YOUR SLAVE or SERVANT) — to the reigning monarch and all *anak2 raja*.

---

\* The words *SILA, PERSILA* or *SILA-KAN* are nowadays used in Johore, for the reigning monarch and all *anak2 raja* only, while for commoners the word *JEMPUT, JEMPUT-KAN* or *JEMPUT-LAH* is used instead.

## B. DRESS REGULATIONS

### Dress Restrictions in the Istana and Balairong

It has been laid down in the *'adat isti'adat diraja Melayu* for generations that while attending ceremonial functions in the *Istana* (Palace) or *Balairong Seri* (Audience Hall or Court) the following dress restrictions must be strictly observed:

(a) No commoner, no matter how highly titled he or she may be, is allowed to wear any dress of yellow or yellowish colour, unless the right to do so is specially granted by the reigning monarch either the *Sultan* or the *Yang Di-Pertuan Besar*. To go against this ruling is to commit a punishable offence.

(b) No commoner may dress in thin and transparent cloth on material, unless he or she is specially granted the right to do so by the *Sultan*. But such restrictions are only imposed at the ceremonies mentioned above.

(c) It is strictly prohibited for anyone, except the *Bendahara*, *Temenggong* and those of royal descent (*anak2 raja*), to wear or use *keris harubi emas sa-bungkal* (*keris* with handle encased in gold weighing one *bungkal*). The punishment for this offence is the confiscation of the *keris* worn or used.

## C. ETIQUETTE OF PAYING HOMAGE TO ROYALTY

1. PROCEDURES TO BE ADOPTED

    (a) When in the audience of the reigning monarch (either the *Sultan* or the *Yang Di-Pertuan Besar*) in the *Balairong* or in any other gathering, the *sembah* (show of obeisance made with both hands close together, as in prayer, with finger-tips touching, the hands then being raised to the forehead) should be directed only to him.

    (b) If in the Throne Hall or in any other gathering, the Crown Prince (either the *Yang Di-Pertuan Muda* or the *Raja Muda*), but not the *Sultan*, is present, then the *sembah* should be directed only to the Crown Prince.

    (c) And if only the *Bendahara* is present, then the *sembah* should be directed only to him. (The *Bendahara* is the most important and highest official in the State and he is also the Prime Minister.)

    (d) Likewise in the absence of the royal persons mentioned above, the *sembah* should be directed to the *Temenggong* (the highest official of the State next to the *Bendahara*).

2. **THE MENYEMBAH** (Act of Showing Obeisance)

It should be performed as follows:

(a) To the reigning monarch: Bring the hands together and, with fingers closed and palms touching, raise them to the forehead until the tips of the thumbs touch the forehead between the eyebrows.

(b) To either the *Yang Di-Pertuan Muda* or the *Raja Muda*: With hands and fingers as above, raise the hands in the same manner, till the tips of the thumbs touch the tip of the nose.

(c) To the *Bendahara* and *Temenggong*: Similarly as above, raise the hands till the tips of the thumbs touch the tip of the chin.

NOTES:

(i) The truly traditional Malay *menyembah* should only be performed while sitting down, and preferably with right knee up and the left leg bent and sat upon. *Menyembah* while standing or working was never known in the *'adat isti'adat diraja Melayu*.

(ii) When performing the *menyembah* to leave the audience of the monarch, do not turn round immediately and leave the place. After performing the *sembah*, get up and step slowly three paces backwards, then sit again in the manner described, and perform the *sembah* as before. Then get up, step again three steps backwards, turn slowly and leave the audience room.

(iii) When talking to or in the presence of royalty, such as the *Yang Di-Pertuan Besar, Sultan,* the *Yang Di-Pertuan Muda, Bendahara* and *Temenggong,* it is traditionally encumbent upon anyone, however high his or her rank or however valiant his deeds, to speak in a soft and most respectful tone of voice — never in a high, angry or rough tone.

## D. PROHIBITION AGAINST IMITATING THE STRUCTURE OF CERTAIN PARTS OF THE PALACE

It is forbidden to reproduce the following buildings or parts of the palace:

(i) *BALAIRONG SERI* (*Sultan's* Audience Hall or Court)

(ii) *SAYAP-LAYANG* (swallow-winged roofing, unsupported by posts, usually jutting out of the front door of the *Istana*)

(iii) *PINTU GERBANG ISTANA* (Palace main gate)

(iv) *TINGKAP PANJANG* (window running the whole length of the verandah of the *Istana*)

(v) *PERBALAIAN* or *GETA* (raised platform-like places in the *Istana*)

(vi) *PERSELASARAN* or *SELASAR* (verandah or gallery as an extension to the Palace porch).

Any of the above may only be imitated with special permission from the *Sultan*.

## E. ETIQUETTE ON PUBLIC ROADS

### 1. WHEN THE MONARCH GOES OUT ON PUBLIC ROADS

Whenever either the *Yang Di-Pertuan Besar* or the *Sultan* goes out on the public roads, a sword-bearer, carrying the royal sword, walks about twenty to thirty feet before the *Sultan*, who is usually followed by his retinue. Anyone meeting the sword-bearer must at once stop and sit by the side of the road until the *Sultan* and his retinue have passed. Disobeying this is a punishable offence, except if the offender is a foreigner, ignorant of the '*adat*, in which case he or she is excused but should be informed of the '*adat*.

### 2. ETIQUETTE OF WALKING ON PUBLIC ROADS

Any man, even though he be of royal descent, or a man of rank, walking along any public road should give the right of way to any of the following whom he may happen to meet:

(i) The *Yang Di-Pertuan Besar* or *Sultan*
(ii) The *Yang Di-Pertuan Muda* or the *Raja Muda*
(iii) The *Bendahara*
(iv) The *Temenggong*

- (v) The *Tengku Besar*
- (vi) Womenfolk — married or single, who are either visiting or returning from a shrine
- (vii) Funeral processions
- (viii) Wedding processions
- (ix) Persons carrying heavy loads or burdens
- (x) Blind persons
- (xi) Children
- (xii) Mad persons.

## F. DUTIES AND RESPONSIBILITIES OF THE PENGHULU ISTANA

The *Penghulu Istana* (Palace Caretaker) should be thoroughly versed in the ancient royal Malay and Bugis customs and traditions, so that he may fulfil his duties and responsibilities, which are as follows:

1. To see to the proper seating of guests, particularly of royalty, in the *Istana* (and, in smaller kingdoms where he is also the *Penghulu Balairong*, the *Balairong* as well) on ceremonial occasions.

- (a) The *anak2 raja* are to be seated at the *perbalaian* (the raised platform) on the right and left sides of the throne in order of precedence.
- (b) The *Raja Perempuan*, *Permaisuri* or *Sultana* (wife of a *Sultan*) is seated at the head of any gathering and given a gold

or silver *jurong* (bowl containing *sireh*-leaves).

(c) Common-born secondary wives of royalty and their children are seated on the left- and right-hand sides in the *tela* (outhouse adjoining the palace), also in order of precedence.

(d) *Datin* (wives of *dato'*), their children and their close relatives, and *anak baik* (people of gentle birth) are put on the left side of the *tela* in order of precedence.

(e) *Hamba2 raja* (slaves or servants of the *Sultan*) are seated in the centre of the *tela*, next to the Bugis women.

(f) The commoners and servants or slaves of well-born persons are seated on the verandah of the palace.

2. To look after the well-being of guests at official functions, and to ensure their correct observance of the *'adat*.

(a) Should anyone be found seated in the wrong place, the *Penghulu Istana* is to call the defaulter quietly aside and advise him. He should display neither force nor harshness either in giving the advice or in showing the right place.

(b) As soon as guests arrive, the *Penghulu Istana* and his assistants should immediately approach, receive and escort them to their respective and rightful positions in the *Istana*.

(c) The *Penghulu Istana* gives leave to any guest who may ask to be excused, and he and his assistants should look after them, directing their steps and assisting any who may feel faint.

3. The *Penghulu Istana* is required to keep track of all that goes on within his jurisdiction and to act accordingly.

(a) When a post falls vacant, or there is a shortage of materials, he should notify the relevant authority.

(b) The *Penghulu* should not permit any act or behaviour which is not proper in the *Istana*. If the perpetrator of such acts puts up arguments to prove that they are in accordance with Malay customs and traditions, and stubbornly persists in his actions the *Penghulu* should immediately report the matter to the authority of the *Istana* so that, if proved guilty, the offender may be suitably punished.

(c) The *Penghulu* should estimate (working on the basis of four or five persons to a tray) the number of *hidangan* (trays of dishes served in a feast) which should be ordered from the *penanggah* (palace kitchen) for a *jamuan* (feast) in the *Istana*.

(d) In the case of any practice not provided for in the *'adat isti'adat* or not known to the *Penghulu*, he should consult the *Dato' Isti'adat*, who is the authority on such matters.

## G. DUTIES AND RESPONSIBILITIES OF THE PENGHULU BALAIRONG SERI

The *Penghulu Balairong Seri* (Superintendent of the *Sultan's* Audience Court) must be thoroughly acquainted with the provisions of the *'adat isti'adat* pertaining to the *Balairong*.

1. He must see to the proper seating of guests in the *Balairong*:

   (a) All members of royalty are seated at the *Seri Balai* (main or top section of the *Balairong*), in the following order of precedence:

   (i) Local *anak2 raja* (princes and princesses) with titles

   (ii) *Anak2 raja* with titles, from outlying countries

   (iii) *Anak2 raja* whose fathers are honoured with titles

   (iv) Ordinary local *anak2 raja*

   (v) Ordinary *anak2 raja* of outlying countries.

   EXCEPTION: Aged *anak2 raja* are not strictly bound by these provisions, because of the respect due to their age.

- (b) *Anak-baik* (people of gentle birth) are seated to the right of the *Balairong*.
- (c) The *Haji* (men who have been on pilgrimage to Mecca) and *lebai* (lower order of priests) are seated to the left of the *Balairong*.
- (d) If those to be seated are of equal rank or status then age should determine precedence.

2. He must ensure that the correct procedure is observed at ceremonial functions.

- (a) *Anak2 raja* of very high rank, for example the *Bendahara* and *Temenggong*, or those who are, by right, entitled to partake of food from one and the same food-tray as the *Yang Di-Pertuan Muda* or *Raja Muda*, may be served each with a gold or silver *jurong*.
- (b) Local *dato'*, such as a *Laksamana* and a *Shahbandar*, may also be served with *kerongkop* (type of receptacle for *sireh*-leaves) and a *pahar* or *semberip* (small pedestalled tray) of food.
- (c) The *Imam* (leader of congregational prayer) of the country may also be served with a *pahar* or *semberip* of food. During the period of reading the *Maulud*

(the birth of Prophet Muhammad) the *Imam* is asked to sit at the end of the *Seri Balai,* together with the *dato'* and the rest of the *'alim* (religious scholars). If there is room, the *Imam* may be permitted to remain there till the end of the ceremony.

(d) When a ceremonial feast is over, the *anak2 raja* and other guests may be asked, if they so wish, to enjoy indoor games and other forms of entertainment so that the *Balairong* should not become quiet and dull. The servants in attendance in the *Balairong* should remain there on duty in rotation.

(e) Any guest in the *Balairong* asking for permission to leave should, on giving a plausible excuse, be allowed to go.

(f) Before food-trays are taken into the *Balairong* or *Istana,* the *Penghulu* should first request all the guests therein to be seated in their respective places.

(g) The etiquette to be adopted by tray-carriers is as follows:
    (i) The trays for the *Seri Balai* (top or main part of the *Balairong*) should be carried in first and placed in order.
    (ii) Then trays for the right section of the *Balai* are brought in next, and on the entry of the first tray for the

right section, the trays in the *Seri Balai* should be uncovered and the chief guests begin eating. (All food-trays in former days had covers.)

(iii) Then the food-trays for the left section of the *Balai* are taken in, and immediately the first tray is carried in, the trays in the right section are uncovered and the guests commence eating.

(iv) After all the trays for the left section of the *Balai* have been brought in, they are uncovered and the guests there start eating.

(v) It is further provided in the *'adat isti'adat diraja* that a tray-carrier should, when putting down or taking away a tray in the *Seri Balai*, face towards the highest titled personage present there.

(vi) Tray-carriers, when putting down or taking away trays in the right and left sections of the *Balai*, should also face towards the *Seri Balai*, notwithstanding the presence of any person of rank, no matter how high, for the *Seri Balai* is the place for the accommodation of *Sultan* and royalty, so due respect is given to it.

3. He must ensure that the *'adat,* etiquette and order of the *Balairong* are preserved and respected.

   (a) Both *Penghulu Balairong* and *Penghulu Istana* should take careful note of all the people who come to the *Balairong* or the *Istana,* lest any be faulty in his or her dress, or be seated in the wrong place. Should they find any such fault, it is the duty of the *Penghulu* to put it right immediately, but it must be done in the mildest and most respectful language and manner. Those found wrongly attired should be courteously called to a quiet and secluded place, where they can be advised in privacy. But in the event of any defaulter being found to be stubborn, even after three warnings, he should then be driven out of the place.

   (b) Rules for the seating of leaders or captains of foreign people and of commoners are not provided for in the *'adat isti'adat,* and they may, therefore, be accommodated on the verandah of the *Balairong* or *Istana.*

   (c) The heads or chiefs of the food-tray carriers, whom the *Penghulu* may select and appoint, are given the freedom to go in and out of the *Balairong* and *Istana* at any time for essential supplies and requirements.

(d) Should there arise any doubt or any point that is not mentioned in the *'adat isti'adat* but that requires clarification, the *Dato' Isti'adat* is the authority from whom to seek advice.

## H. ISTI'ADAT SUDUN

(THE RIGHT TO EAT TOGETHER FROM THE SAME TRAY)

On this subject, the *'adat isti'adat diraja Melayu* gives the following traditional rules:

(a) Those who are entitled to partake of food from one and the same *hidangan* (a tray of dishes) are the *Yang Di-Pertuan Muda, Raja Muda* (Crown Prince) and *Bendahara*. No one else may eat from the same tray, except with the expressed order or permission of the *Sultan*. But it should be noted that this *'adat* is not applicable in any gathering or function other than those ceremonially held in the *Balairong* or *Istana*.

(b) Children of the *Yang Di-Pertuan Muda, Raja Muda,* and of the *Bendahara* may eat together from one and the same tray — in fact there is no very strict ruling for them in the *Balairong* and none, of course, in other places.

EXCEPTIONS:
1. Aged *raja* (members of royal families) are not very strictly bound by 'adat, out of respect for their age.
2. Very young *anak2 raja* are also exempted, unless the 'adat is enforced for their education and training.

CHAPTER TWO

# THE NOBAT (ROYAL BAND)

THE following are the rules under the Royal Malay Customs and Traditions, governing the beating or playing of the *Nobat* (Royal Band). These rules were determined on the 25th day of *Sha'aban* in the year of the *Hijrah* 1274, by His Majesty the *Yang Di-Pertuan Besar*, Almarhum Sultan Sulaiman Badrul 'Alam Shah, when he was proclaimed *Sultan* and *Yang Di-Pertuan Besar* of Rhio Lingga and all its dependencies (including Johore, Selangor, and Pahang), and these rules under the '*adat* were not supposed to be amended, augmented, omitted, or altered in any other way:

1. There are certain customs concerning the show of respect which is due to the sound of the *Nobat*, and thus, symbolically to the ruling monarch himself.

(a) Immediately a person hears the sound of the *nepiri* (a flute-like instrument, the principal and most honoured musical instrument of the *Nobat*), no matter from how far away the sound may come, he must stop what he is doing and sit down, with great respect, as though he were in the presence of his sovereign, and he must remain so until the end of the third blowing of the *nepiri,* when he may get up and proceed on his journey. Anyone ignoring this custom commits an act of disrespect to his sovereign, but this neglect is not punishable as an offence. But if anyone should cross or pass in front of the *nepiri* while the *Nobat* is being played outside the compound of the Palace, then he or she is committing a punishable offence.

(b) If a person is walking inside the *Kota* (compound of the Palace or *Balairong*) and suddenly hears the sound of the *nepiri,* he or she must at once sit and bow down to show respect as if in the presence of the sovereign. After three repeated blasts of the *nepiri,* comes the *guroh* (drumming sound) of the *nengkara* (kettle-drum) of the *Nobat* and at the end of this drumming, the person may lift his head, but not stand or move. He has to wait until the end of the third drumming of the *nengkara* before he may get up and go on his way. Anyone disobeying this rule is punishable by a fine of *enam suku* (six quarters or one dollar and fifty cents), imposed by the Chief or *Penghulu Nobat* himself.

2. The only four personages for whom the *Nobat* may be played are:

(i) The ruling monarch, the *Yang Di-Per-*

*tuan Besar* or the *Sultan*

(ii) The Crown Prince, the *Yang Di-Pertuan Muda* or the *Raja Muda* or *Putera Mahkota*

(iii) The *Bendahara*

(iv) The *Temenggong*.

Absolutely no one, other than the above four personages, is entitled to the beating of the *Nobat*, except by special permission from the *Sultan*.

3. The *Nobat* plays for the different personages as follows:

(a) For the ruling monarch, a period equal to thirty-two blasts of the *nepiri*

(b) For the *Yang Di-Pertuan Muda*, a period equal to not more than eleven blasts of the *nepiri*

(c) For the *Bendahara*, nine blasts

(d) For the *Temenggong*, seven blasts.

4. It is to be noted that no one is permitted to reproduce the *Nobat* as a whole, nor any one of its instruments, particularly the *nepiri*, without the express command of the *Yang Di-Pertuan Besar* himself; for the *Nobat* is, according to the Royal Malay Customs and Traditions, an emblem of kingship, showing that there is a monarch reigning in the country. Even the *Yang Di-Pertuan Muda* is not allowed to ask for the *Nobat* or even for any of its instruments to be made, without the express injunction of the *Yang Di-Pertuan Besar*,

unless it be on the occasion of the accession of the *Yang Di-Pertuan Besar* to the Throne. Even then what the *Yang Di-Pertuan Muda* may make or order to be made are only the *gendang* and *nengkara* (drum) and the *serunai* (flute) but not the *nepiri*. The *Yang Di-Pertuan Muda* may only repair or replace any part of the *nepiri* that is damaged or is out of order.

5. The regulation tunes played by the *Nobat* are governed by the occasion. The two most important are:

   (a) The *lagu* (tune) "*Ibrahim Khalilullah*" which is played for the ruling monarch alone, during the *Tabal* (ceremonies of installation) and *Menjunjong Duli* (paying obeisance to the monarch).

   (b) The *lagu* "*Iskandar Shah Zulqarnain*" (commonly known as either "*Arak Arak*" or "*Lagu Ria*" and usually followed by "*Lagu Perang*") is played while the *Sultan* is escorted in procession on his way, for example, from the *Istana* to the *Balairong* (Audience Hall).

Other tunes besides the above two are all fairly new tunes, taken from Perak and Indragiri, with variations not specifically mentioned here as none of them was accepted for the exaltation of kingship. They were merely additions to the repertoire of *Nobat* tunes.

6. The procedure for the *Nobat*, the different

occasions on which, and the personages for whom, it performs, are as follows:

(a) The *Nobat* performs every evening up to the time of *Maghrib* Prayer (the fourth Muslim prayer of the day at about 7 p.m.). When the *Nobat* is due to start playing, the *Penghulu Gendang* (chief *gendang*-beater), called *Leila Sengguna,* summons the band. He sounds a token beating on the *gendang* and then stops a while. When it is time to start, all the players come forward and line up, standing in their proper places. The chief of the *Nobat*, called *Leila Perkasa,* whose duty is to blow the highly-honoured *nepiri*, stands in the front by himself. Immediately behind him in line stand the two *nengkara* (royal kettle-drum) players. In the third line, behind the *nengkara*, stand the beaters of one big *gendang* (big drum) and two *gendang2 peningkah* (smaller common drums) with *Leila Sengguna* as their leader. In the fourth line stand the two blowers of the two types of pipes, called respectively *serunai* and *bangsi*. In the fifth and last line stand the rest of the band, that is, the beaters of the *kopak* (a sort of tambourine) and *cherachap* (a percussion instrument comprising two pieces of bamboo). When members of the *Nobat* have taken their positions and are ready, the *Leila Perkasa* (leader of the *Nobat*) then blows the *nepiri* three times. This is immediately followed by the drumming of the *nengkara*, also three times. Then comes the beating of all the *gendang*, and following this the *nengkara* makes the second drumming sound (*guroh*). Only then does the *Nobat* commence to play the required tune. The maximum period the *Nobat* may play is the time it takes the *nepiri* to complete its thirty-two blasts. Then the performance is terminated by sounding the war beats on the *gendang*.

(b) On *Malam Juma'at* (Thursday evening) at the time of the *'Isha* prayer (the fifth prayer of the day at about 8 p.m.) the *Nobat* plays any tune other than that of the early morning prayer.

(c) The "*Ibrahim Khalilullah*" tune is only played during the ceremonies of *Tabal* (accession to the throne) and *Menjunjong Duli* (obeisance to the *Sultan*) and the "*Iskandar Shah*", also known as the "*Arak Arak*", is the royal processional tune played when the *Sultan* is on his way to and from the *Balairong*, *Balai Panchapersada* (tiered bathing pavilion), and *Istana*.

(d) Besides these two special tunes, a few others are played during the Installation Ceremonies. *"Palu-Palu"* is played when the monarch is bathing at the *Panchapersada*, and *"Seri Istana"* is played while he is putting on his royal robes of State.

(e) While preparations for the bathing ceremony are being made at the *Panchapersada* the *Nobat* plays *"Lagu Perang"*. This tune is also played annually on the morning of *Hari Raya Haji* (feast day commemorating the end of the pilgrimage to Mecca).

(f) When the *Sultan* starts for the *Panchapersada* in procession, the *Nobat* plays the tune *"Arak-Arak"*. On his arrival at the bathing place, the *Nobat* stops for a little while, after which the *nepiri* is blown three times, followed immediately by the *Nobat* playing *lagu "Palu-Palu"*. After the ceremonial bath, the Sultan returns to the *Istana* again to the strains of the processional *"Arak Arak"*. The *Nobat* changes to the tune *"Seri Istana"*, while the *Sultan* is donning his royal robes of State, and stops beating when the *Sultan* has finished dressing.

(g) The *Sultan* then proceeds to the *Balairong* for the ceremony of *Menjunjong Duli* (paying homage to the monarch).

The *Nobat* plays the *"Arak Arak"* again, until the monarch is seated on the *Singgahsana* (throne), when they strike up the *"Ibrahim Khalilullah"*, the royal tune of the kingdom. It is absolutely forbidden to play this tune for any other than the ruling monarch of the kingdom. After the *Menjunjong Duli* ceremony, the *Sultan* returns to the *Istana*, once more accompanied by the processional *"Arak Arak"*.

(h) The traditional *adab* (formation) of the *Nobat* players standing in ordained lines is only obligatory when the tunes *"Ibrahim Khalilullah"* and *"Iskandar Shah"* are played.

(i) When playing the tune *"Seri Istana"*, or when playing while the *Sultan* is bathing at the *Panchapersada* during the accession ceremony, the players may sit down, but in exactly the same order as while standing. For other tunes, it is left to the discretion of the *Leila Perkasa* (Chief of the *Nobat*) and *Leila Sengguna* (Chief of the *Gendang*) to determine which procedure to adopt.

These are the procedures for *Nobat* performances, reconstructed as best the author can, from memory, from such records as he was able to obtain, and from information given by aged Malays with knowledge of these matters.

The explanation is detailed and occupies a chapter of its own because the *Nobat* played a most important port in royal ceremonies, and was highly exalted. The *Nobat* was very much more honoured by the Malays of old and meant very much more to them than the State Band does to the present-day Malays.

CHAPTER THREE

# RULES GOVERNING MARRIAGE

## A. DOWRY AND EXPENSES

### 1. For Ruling Monarchs

In a marriage between the ruling *Sultan* or *Raja* and the daughter of another reigning monarch, the following are the *maskahwin* (dowry), the marriage expenses, and materials to be offered to the bride:

(i) Dowry: one *kati* of gold

(ii) Marriage expenses: eight hundred dollars*

(iii) *Chindai emas* (a certain fabric with gold flowers), sixteen trays of eight pieces per tray*

(iv) *Kain berantai* (chain-patterned *sarong*), sixteen trays of four pieces per tray*

(v) *Kain bertabur* (scatter-patterned *sarong*), sixteen trays of four pieces per tray*

---

\* Half the amount or number, if the couple are closely related.

(vi) *Kain telepok* (*sarong* adorned with tinsel), sixteen trays of four pieces per tray*

(vii) *Kain Bugis* (Bugis-woven *sarong*), four score, in sixteen trays of five pieces per tray*

(viii) *Kain sutera* (silk *sarong*) four score, in sixteen trays of five pieces per tray*

(ix) *Kain batek* (batik *sarong*), four score in sixteen trays of five pieces per tray*

(x) *Khasa bunga emas* (muslin cloth with gold flowers), one hundred and twenty-eight *kayu* in sixteen trays of eight *kayu* per tray*

(xi) Sixteen *budak2 dapa* (slave-messengers) bearing gifts that accompany the marriage proposal. They are also kept as part of the gifts — they are eight boys and eight girls*

(xii) Eight diamond rings of eight carat each*.

Each of the above items, except the sixteen *budak2 dapa*, is to be borne by a special carrier and accompanying the carriers are the following *penjawat* (palace officials with special duties in the royal service):

(a) Sixteen *Penjawat2 Kain-Dukong* (officials wearing ceremonial neck-cloth)

(b) One *Penjawat Keris* (official carrying a *keris*)

(c) One *Penjawat Tepak* (official carrying a *sireh*-box)

(d) One *Penjawat Ketor* (official carrying a spittoon).

All the above carriers, except the one carrying the dowry, and all *penjawat* are to wear *wali* (WHITE ceremonial cloth) which must dangle from the RIGHT shoulder. The man carrying the dowry wears a *tetampan* (YELLOW ceremonial cloth) which must dangle from the LEFT shoulder.

2. PROPER ORDER OF THE PROCESSION CARRYING THE DOWRY, ETC.

The article carried at the head of the procession is the dowry, and the *belanja* (wedding expenses) of eight hundred dollars comes immediately after. Then comes the bridegroom *berjulang* (borne on men's shoulders as a mark of respect) under a big yellow *payong ubor* (umbrella of royalty). He is followed by the rest of the *hantaran* (things sent) in the following order:

(i) Trays of *chindai emas*
(ii) Trays of *khasa bunga emas*
(iii) Trays of *kain berantai*

(iv) Trays of *kain bertabur*
(v) Trays of *kain telepok*
(vi) Trays of *kain Bugis*
(vii) Trays of *kain sutera*
(viii) Trays of *kain batek*
(ix) The sixteen *budak2 dapa* — eight boys and eight girls
(x) The gold receptacle containing the eight diamond rings
(xi) Sixteen *Penjawat2 Kain-Dukong* (special palace officials with royal stoles dangling from their necks), eight on each side of the bridegroom
(xii) One *Penjawat Keris*
(xiii) One *Penjawat Tepak*
(xiv) One *Penjawat Ketor*.

Then follows a man carrying the Spear of Royalty, and just behind this come sixteen spear-bearers in two lines — eight on each side. Behind these two lines of spear-bearers comes the *Nobat*.

As soon as the royal procession begins, the *Nobat* plays and the first of sixteen gunshots are fired. These shots are spaced at intervals, so that the sound of the last shot marks the arrival of the procession.

NOTE:

Very often the ceremony for the solemnisation of the marriage, called *'akad*, takes place on the same day that the dowry and marriage expenses are sent. It is only under these circumstances that the bridegroom accompanies the procession.

3. **DOWRIES AND EXPENSES OF ORDINARY ANAK2 RAJA AND OTHERS**

   (a) For ordinary *anak2 raja*, the dowry is four hundred dollars (mentioned in the register as one *kati* of gold). The *hantaran* (articles sent with the dowry) is agreed upon by the two parties concerned.
   (b) For the widow of a *Sultan*, one hundred dollars, a ring (usually diamond) and one *sarong*.
   (c) For women of the *Istana*, forty-four dollars, a ring and one *sarong*.
   (d) For daughters of *Dato'*, one hundred dollars, a ring and one *sarong*.
   (e) Descendants of Bugis, forty-eight dollars, a ring and one *sarong*.
   (f) Bugis maidens of gentle birth, sixty dollars, a ring and one *sarong*.
   (g) Other maidens associated with the *Istana* forty-one dollars, a ring and one *sarong*.

B. ORDER OF THE ROYAL WEDDING PROCESSION

If the ʻ*akad* does not take place on the same day that the dowry is sent, the wedding procession moves in the following order:
1. At the head of the procession walks a group of the leading ladies of the bridegroom's side.

2. Next comes a party of *zikir* singers (people singing in praise of the Prophet Muhammad) beating *rebana* (a type of timbrel).
3. Then comes the *Nobat*, flanked on each side by eight either spear-or rifle-bearers, sixteen in all.
4. They are followed by the official with the *Tombak Kerajaan* (Spear of State).
5. Behind him come various other officials. One, the *Penjawat Puan*, carries the ceremonial betel-bowl, and others, *Penjawat2 Bungkusan*, carry bundles of raiment.
6. Now comes the *Usongan Diraja* (the royal hammock-litter) bearing the royal bridegroom (sometimes the bride as well) and his attendants —
   (i) *Penjawat Keris Panjang*, with a long *keris*
   (ii) *Penjawat Tepak*, with the ceremonial *sireh*-box
   (iii) *Penjawat Ketor*, with a spittoon
   (iv) *Penjawat Ternang*, with a gold or silver water-bowl.

   Each of these *penjawat* wears, on his left shoulder, a *tetampan*.

   The *Usongan Diraja* is beautifully decorated, and is curtained with fine silk—yellow if the bridegroom is either *Yang Di-Pertuan Besar* or *Sultan*, green if he is the *Yang Di-Pertuan Muda* (Crown Prince).

The *usongan* is also sheltered on all sides by either four or eight large *payong ubor* (ceremonial umbrellas).

7. Sixteen *Penjawat2 Kain-Dukong* walk alongside the *Usongan Diraja*, eight on either side, they all wear *tetampan* on the left shoulder.
8. Finally, in the rear of the procession comes a host of musicians.

Immediately the royal procession starts to move, the first shot of a salute of sixteen, nine or seven guns is fired to indicate the commencement. When the procession reaches its destination, the last shot indicates the reception by the royal bride of her bridegroom.

CHAPTER FOUR

# TABALKAN
# (INSTALLATION OF A MONARCH)

*NOTE: This refers to the installation as monarch of one of the following three persons:*
*(1) The Yang Di-Pertuan Besar*
*(2) The Yang Di-Pertuan Muda*
*(3) The Bendahara*

1. PREPARATIONS FOR THE TABALKAN

AFTER the princes, ministers, *dato'* and other high officials of State have conferred and unanimously decided on the day and time of the Installation Ceremony, instructions are sent out to clean up the country, and rebuild walls, roads and bridges. Special and urgent instructions are sent out by the *Bendahara* to prepare the *Istana, Balairong* and *Balai Panchapersada* (tiered bathing pavilion) for the great occasion. Markets, bazaars and shops are repaired, some are enlarged, and some new ones are built to meet the needs of the occasion. The *ra'ayat* (the people) all over the country are informed of the occasion of the accession to the throne of the new *Sultan* or *Yang Di-Pertuan Besar*. Letters of announcement and invitations to relatives living outstation and abroad are sent. Official invitations to rulers of dependent countries, with the special request to bring their families and relatives, are all despatched early.

When all this has been done, the ministers, *dato'* and some others of gentle birth go into the *perdalaman* (the confines of the *Istana*) to prepare and decorate the *Istana*, the *Balairong* and the *Balai Panchapersada*. All pillars are draped with royal cloth or painted yellow, and throughout the inside of the *Istana* and the two *Balai*, beautiful and colourful decorations are put up.

## 2. Commencement of the Installation Ceremony

When all is ready, the *Yang Di-Pertuan Muda* or the *Bendahara* publicly announces the commencement of the Ceremony of Installation. Then the princes and princesses, ministers, *dato'* and *datin* and all the state dignitaries are welcomed into the *perdalaman* (inside the *Kota*). From this moment, the *Nobat* plays regularly seven times daily, and feasting, entertainment and games of all sorts begin and continue for forty-four days and nights throughout the capital of the country.

From the hour of the day the ceremony officially starts, the provisions of the *'adat isti'adat diraja* concerning dress, seating, etc., in both the *Balairong* and in the *Istana*, are strictly enforced. The enforcement of these provisions is usually carried out in the most careful manner, and strictly in accordance with the *'adat*. Two *Penghulu* are officially appointed, one for the *Balai* and one for the *Istana*. They are men of either royal blood or gentle birth, well-versed in the requirements of the *'adat isti'adat diraja* and able to see to its proper and just enforcement.

These *Penghulu* are given full authority and made fully responsible for the management of affairs in the *Balairong* and in the *Istana*, particularly during ceremonial functions.

### 3. Duties and Responsibilities of the Penghulu Istana During the Installation Ceremony

At the command of the *Yang Di-Pertuan Muda* or *Bendahara*, the *Penghulu Istana* is to commence seeing to the imposition of the provisions of the *'adat isti'adat*, and the *Penghulu* is himself, from that instant, to start wearing the traditional *Penghulu's* attire, that is, the *baju pandak* (short coat), if he is not of royal blood, or if of royalty, *baju takua* (a long coat with narrow sleeves). He is to wear a gold chain round his wrist as a token of his authority and office, and no one is to disregard his bidding. To assist him during ceremonial functions, a number of experienced men are appointed to be his assistants.

4. SERVERS OR PENJAWAT DURING THE INSTALLATION CEREMONY

The following servers are essentially required:

(a) Sixteen *penjawat2 kain-dukong* are at all times required to follow the *Sultan* wherever he goes. When the *Sultan* is at the *Balai Panchapersada*, they are to take their places on the second tier of the *Balai*, a little towards the back of the *Singgahsana*. When the *Sultan* is at the *Istana* or at the *Balairong*, they sit in rows just behind the *Singgahsana*, on the first tier.

(b) Besides these *penjawat*, there are sixteen others specially required for the Installation Ceremony (*Tabal*), and they should all be *anak2 raja* — eight princes and eight princesses — and each one of them *menyelampai* (wear dangling on the LEFT shoulder) a *tetampan* (ceremonial YELLOW shoulder cloth). They derive their official titles from the articles which they carry, and they come in the following order—

The male *penjawat* each carries:

(i) A *pedang* (sword) — *Penjawat Pedang*

- (ii) A *chogan* (standard or metallic emblem) — *Penjawat Chogan*
- (iii) A *keris panjang* (long *keris*) — *Penjawat Keris Panjang*
- (iv) A *tepak* (*sireh*-box) — *Penjawat Tepak*
- (v) A *ketor* (spittoon) — *Penjawat Ketor*
- (vi) A *kipas* (fan) — *Penjawat Kipas*
- (vii) A *tempat-bara* (incense-burner) — *Penjawat Tempat-Bara*
- (viii) The Quran — *Penjawat Quran*.

Similarly, each of the female *penjawat* carries:

- (i) A *ternang* (water-jug or -bowl) — *Penjawat Ternang*
- (ii) A *kembok* (another type of water-bowl) — *Penjawat Kembok*
- (iii) A *semberap* (a tray with a complete set of containers for incense, rose-water, etc.) — *Penjawat Semberap*
- (iv) A *tepak* (*sireh*-box) — *Penjawat Tepak*
- (v) A *ketor* (spittoon) — *Penjawat Ketor*
- (vi) An *embat-embat* (a hollow receptacle for sprinkling rose-water) — *Penjawat Embat-Embat*
- (vii) A *cheper berteh* (a tray of parched rice) — *Penjawat Cheper Berteh*
- (viii) A *cheper beras kunyit* (a tray of yellow rice) — *Penjawat Beras Kunyit*.

The services of female *penjawat* are only required at the *Balai Panchapersada* when the Installation Bathing Ceremony is held and in the *Istana* when the *Sultan santap* (eats), while the services of the male *penjawat* are required when the *Sultan* is at the *Balairong* and when he is on his way to and from the *Istana*, *Balairong* and *Balai Panchapersada*. At the *Balai Panchapersada* and *Istana*, the male *penjawat* hand over the articles they carry to the female *penjawat*.

5. REGULATIONS FOR THE BEATING OF THE NOBAT DURING THE INSTALLATION CEREMONY

In addition to playing at the commencement of the ceremony, the *Nobat* then performs regularly seven times during a night and a day, namely:

(a) Every afternoon at about 5 p.m. till *maghrib* (first prayer of the night)
(b) At the time of the 'Isha Prayer (second prayer of the night)
(c) At the time of the *Suboh* Prayer (first morning prayer)
(d) When the *Sultan* takes his *santapan tengah hari* (lunch)
(e) When the *Sultan* leaves the *Istana* for the *Balairong*
(f) When the *Sultan* returns from the *Balairong* to the *Istana*

(g) When the *Sultan* goes in to *beradu* (sleep).

As soon as the *Nobat* stops playing, the gun is fired and *gemalan* (Javanese orchestras) start to play.

6. COMMENCEMENT OF THE
    INSTALLATION PROCESSION

(a) When the *Sultan* begins to put on his official attire, the *Nobat* starts to play the tune "*Seri Istana*".
(b) When completely dressed, the *Sultan* gets onto the *Usongan* (litter), which is decked with royal yellow silk and is beautifully decorated.
(c) A *pedang*-bearer (sword-bearer) proceeds in front of the *Usongan*.
(d) *Penjawat* carrying the following articles accompany the *Sultan* on the *Usongan*:
  (i) *Chogan* (standard)
  (ii) *Keris*
  (iii) *Ketor* (spittoon)
  (iv) *Beras kunyit* (yellow rice).
(e) Two old *anak2 raja* — one standing at the front and the other at the rear of the *Usongan* act as chiefs of the *Usongan*.
  (All these attendants on the *Usongan* wear *tetampan* on their shoulders.)
(f) Eight (or four) other *penjawat* each wearing a *wali* (white ceremonial shoulder-cloth for

the right shoulder) sit in line facing the *Sultan* who is on the dais.

(g) At each of the four corners of the *Usongan* stands a young person, who throws or scatters about handfuls of yellow rice mixed with chips of gold and silver to the public all along the way of the procession. As soon as the procession starts to move, the eight *payong ubor* (big royal umbrellas) — four of royal yellow and four of white — immediately open to shelter the *Usongan* throughout the journey.

(h) The members of the *Nobat*, in proper order, proceed in front of the *Usongan*, on each side of which march four spear-bearers.

(i) Between the *Nobat* and the *Usongan* walks a carrier of the *Tombak Kerajaan* (Spear of State).

(j) Immediately behind the *Usongan* come sixteen *Dian*-bearers or *Penjawat2 Dian* — eight on each side.

(k) Behind the *Usongan* between the two lines of *Dian*-bearers, walk sixteen *Penjawat2 Kain-Dukong*.

(l) Behind the *Penjawat2 Kain-Dukong* come sixteen or eight *biduan* (singers).

(m) A crowd of people follows right behind the *biduan*.

(n) Lastly come parties of *keromong*, *gemalan* and parties of other musicians.

## 7. Procession to the Balai Panchapersada and Return to the Istana

Immediately the procession starts to move on its way, the *Nobat* commences to play the tune "*Iskandar Shah*" and a salute of seven, nine, or sixteen guns is fired, at intervals long enough for the last shot to be fired on the arrival of the procession at the *Balai Panchapersada* (tiered bathing pavilion). Immediately the procession arrives there the *Nobat* changes to the "*Perang*" tune and repeats the tune until all the *penjawat* and the rest of the important people in the procession have taken their proper places inside and outside the *Balai*.

The *Sultan* then undergoes the ritual of the Installation Token Bathing, and at the same moment the *Nobat* changes its tune to that of "*Palu-palu*".

## 8. Balai Panchapersada

This is the pavilion where the usual royal bathing ceremony for Installation or Marriage is held. It is made of wood and is usually nine tiers high (in accordance with olden Malay '*adat isti'adat*). Each tier is made differently from the others.

The top tier is made with a canopy, supported by four pillars. To each pillar is attached a handmade dragon of wood with some sort of mechanical attachment, by the manipulation of which, one dragon will spout fresh water, the second, lukewarm water, the third, fragrant water of *khalembak* (fragrant wood) and of *kesturi* (musk), and the fourth, *ayer mawar* (rose-water). On this first tier, under the canopy, is placed a *Singgahsana* with four posts. A *selembayong* (square frame with an up-turned crocket at each corner — an emblem of royalty), which is draped with royal yellow silk, is hung over the *Singgahsana*. At each of the four posts of the *Singgahsana* stands a young man or girl of royal blood, each wearing a *tetampan* embroidered with gold thread. If it is a royal wedding and both the *Sultan* and *Sultana* (the bridegroom and bride) are present, then at the posts will stand two young men and two young women of good family. If only the *Sultan* is present, then at the posts will stand four young men. If only the *Sultana* or *Raja Perempuan* is enthroned on the *Singgahsana*, then the four at the posts should be women only. On the *peterakna* (dais) of the *Singgahsana* is placed a bench or stool, completely draped with royal yellow silk, and on this sits the *Sultan* (or both the royal groom and his bride) during the ceremony.

Arrangements for seating in the *Balai Panchapersada* follow a strict ruling:

(a) On the topmost tier is seating accommodation only for the *Sultan* (or for the royal couple) with his female *penjawat* and a very few aged princesses of note.

(b) On the second tier (working downwards) is accommodation for princesses closely related to the installed *Sultan*.

(c) On the third tier sit other princesses.

(d) On the fourth tier, the wives of ministers and their close female relatives.

(e) On the fifth tier, widows of princes and ladies of honoured families.

(f) On the sixth tier, the maids of the *Istana*.

(g) On the seventh tier, wives of *penghulu* and officials together with their close relatives.

(h) On the eighth tier, the women from inside the *Kota Raja* (walled area of the palace).

(i) On the ninth tier, any women of the common people.

NOTE:

Strictly in accordance with the Malay royal customs and traditions, no male person, other than the *Sultan* undergoing the bathing ceremony and the four or two standing at the four posts of the *Singgahsana*, is allowed in the *Balai Panchapersada* during the ceremony.

9. POSITIONS OF PENJAWAT AND OTHER BEARERS AT THE PANCHAPERSADA DURING THE CEREMONY

(a) The sixteen *Penjawat2 Kain-Dukong* are arranged in two lines on the second tier of the

*Panchapersada,* a little to the back of the *Singgahsana* which is on the first tier.

(b) The sixteen *Penjawat2 Dian* (candle-bearers) are placed on the third tier with sixteen or eight *biduan* (sweet-voiced singers) sitting immediately behind them.

(c) On the ground, surrounding the *Balai Panchapersada* stand a line of men bearing *pedang* (swords).

(d) Behind them is a row of men bearing *lembing* (spears with ridged blades).

(e) The third and the last row, is a line of men with bows and arrows.

The three lines are spaced according to the ground available.

In the intervening space, between the *Balai Panchapersada* and the encircling row of sword-bearers, chairs are placed before the front entrance of the *Balai* to seat the Crown Prince and aged princes who are relatives of the installed *Sultan.* In the rest of the intervening space stand groups of young princes.

10. REGULATIONS GOVERNING THE PENJAWAT2 KAIN-DUKONG, BIDUAN (SWEET-VOICED SINGERS), AND PENJAWAT2 DIAN (CANDLE-BEARERS)

(a) *The Penjawat2 Kain-Dukong,* sixteen in number, are to keep themselves in readiness to follow the *Sultan* wherever he goes during the period of the Installation Ceremony. At the *Balai Panchapersada* these *Penjawat2 Kain-Dukong* sit on the second tier, to the back of the *Singgahsana* which is on the first storey. At both the *Istana* and the *Balairong* they sit in lines behind the *Singgahsana*.

(b) The *Dian*-carriers or *Penjawat2 Dian*, sixteen in number, are accommodated in the *Balai Panchapersada* on the right and left sides of the third tier of the *Balai*. When in the *Istana*, they sit in the centre between two *perbalaian* (place with raised platforms), and when following the *Usongan* (hammock-litter) they walk in lines of eight on the right and left sides of the litter.

(c) The number of *biduan* (sweet-voiced singers) required during the Installation Ceremony is eight or sixteen and when in the *Istana* they are accommodated at the *rembah* (an open space separating the main building, which contains the royal rooms, from the rest of the *Istana*). When the *Sultan* goes to the *Balairong* or *Balai Panchapersada*, they follow him walking behind the *dian*-bearers. On arrival at the *Balairong* they stand by the side of the *Peseban* (Hall), but on arriving at the *Balai Panchapersada* they are seated behind the *dian*-bearers on the third tier of the *Balai*.

## 11. Return to the Istana

When the ceremonial bath is over, the *Nobat* again changes its tune to that of *"Arak-Arak"*, and the gun starts firing again to accompany the royal procession back to the *Istana*.

In the *Istana*, the *Yang Di-Pertuan Besar* designate changes into the royal attire of State, and while he is dressing, the *Nobat* accompanies with the tune *"Seri Istana"*. When he is ready, the *Sultan* is again taken on the *Usongan* and in the same procession to the *Balairong Seri*.

## 12. Balairong Seri

The *Balai* is the Royal Audience Hall or Court of the Palace. For the occasion, it is elegantly furnished and decorated, with all its pillars and posts draped with royal yellow silk. Inside the Hall are hung several beautiful curtains, and at the *Seri Balai* (head of the Hall) is hung a screen or curtain on which mountain scenes are drawn or painted. Immediately in front of this is the *Singgahsana*, on which is placed the *peterakna* (dais). A little towards the back of this is placed a *bantal seraga* (round and ornate cushion used at weddings and other ceremonies). It is on the *peterakna* that the *Sultan* sits to receive the obeisance made by his people. Thus also in the *Istana* are the *Singgahsana* and *pelamin* (bridal couch) prepared and decorated.

13. SEATING ARRANGEMENTS AND DRESS DURING THE INSTALLATION

(a) *Raja2 perempuan* or *Permaisuri* (Queens or *Sultana*) are not, during that period in the *Istana*, to wear any token or emblem of titles or appointments hanging from the shoulder or neck, be it a stole or handkerchief.

(b) *Anak2 raja perempuan* (princesses) throughout the period of installation must wear *baju pandak* (short coat) of plain cloth. They may wear silk *baju* (as long as they are of unpatterned material), wristlets and bangles, *pending* (embossed gold or silver clasps for girdles, worn mostly by women), rings, and buttons on the sleeves as well as on the coat neck.

On arrival at the door of the *tela* (outhouse adjoining the palace) all female guests are to take off their *kain kelumbong* or *tudong* (*sarong* used by a Malay lady as a shawl for covering herself from head down to the waist). They hand them over to their maids, who are to keep them on their laps throughout the period of the ceremony, and return them to their mistresses at the same door when they leave the *Istana*.

(c) As soon as the princes and princesses arrive, the *Penghulu* is to order his assistants to receive them immediately with the utmost respect. But if the princess or prince who arrives is one of very high rank, then it is the *Penghulu* himself who is to go and receive her or him. All the guests on arrival are to enter immediately, and to take their respective places as provided for according to rank. Princesses are seated on the right and left sides of the *Singgahsana*.

(d) Secondary wives of *anak2 raja* (princes) are accommodated on the right and left sides of the *tela* according to their rank.

(e) *Datin* (wives of *dato'*) together with their close relatives and people of gentle birth (*anak baik*) are seated on the left side of the *tela*.

(f) Servants and maids of the *Sultan* from the *Istana* are seated in the middle of the *tela*, next to Bugis ladies.

(g) Commoners and servants of people of gentle birth are accommodated in the *serambi* (front portion of the balcony of the *Balai*).

## 14. MENTAULIAH (THE GRANTING OF AUTHORITY) AND MENJUNJONG DULI (OBEISANCE)

(a) On arrival at the *Balairong Seri* the *Sultan* designate is received by the *Yang Di-Pertuan Muda* and seated on the throne. All the royal *penjawat*, the retinue, princes, *mentri* (ministers), *dato'* and the rest of the State officials stand in their places in accordance with their rank. As soon as all are in their places, the *Nobat* plays the tune "*Ibrahim Khalilullah*" — (this tune can be played only for the *Yang Di-Pertuan Besar* or *Sultan* and for no one else, according to the true *'adat isti'adat diraja Melayu*).

(b) The *Yang Di-Pertuan Muda*, with all the ministers and officials of State, stands on the left side of the *Seri Balai* (top or main section of the *Balai*) while foreign dignitaries, if any, stand on the right side of the *Seri Balai*. When everything is ready, the *Yang Di-Pertuan Muda*, followed immediately behind by an *'alim* (religious scholar), comes forward to the *Singgahsana*, pays the usual obeisance and says: "*Daulat Tuanku* (Long Live the Sultan). We, members of *Anlil-hal wal-'akad* (members of the Royal *Dewan*) do hereby authorise and appoint and make Your Majesty, the *Sultan* and *Yang Di-Pertuan Besar* in this Kingdom of...with all its dependencies. And we do all sincerely and solemnly hope that Your Majesty will loyally and solemnly obey the Command of Allah and the bidding of his Prophet and Messenger, as are embodied in the Holy Quran and Sayings of the Prophet Muhammad — may the blessing of Allah be upon him." At the word "Quran" the *Yang Di-Pertuan Muda* points with his right hand to the Holy Quran on the lap of the royal *penjawat* sitting near the *Sultan*. As soon as the *Yang Di-Pertuan Muda* finishes saying the *Tauliah*, the *'alim* lifts both his hands and reads the *do'a selamat* (thanksgiving) and when the *do'a* ends, all those present inside as well as outside the *Balairong* shout in unison *"Daulat Tuanku"* ("Long Live the King") three times. During the delivery of the *Tauliah*, the *Nobat* stops playing, and all listen in silence to the *Yang Di-Pertuan Muda*.

(c) Then, headed by the *Yang Di-Pertuan Muda*, the assembly leaves the *Balairong* for another *Balai* facing it, leaving behind the newly proclaimed *Sultan* with his *penjawat* and two *bentara* (heralds). On reaching the other *Balai*, the *Yang Di-Pertuan Muda* stands on a *tikar pajar* (specially woven mat for royal use) facing the *Balairong*, and behind him stand in rows the rest of the princes, ministers, *dato'* and other officials of the State and others of honoured families.

(d) As soon as the change-over is completed, the *Nobat* strikes up the royal tune *"Ibrahim Khalilullah"*, and a *bentara* (herald) comes out from the *Balairong* to the *Yang Di-Pertuan Muda*, and sits to *menyembah* (make obeisance). He then says:

*"Ampun, Tuanku Yang Di-Pertuan Muda* (Forgive me, Your Highness), *Yang Maha Mulia, titah mempersilakan Tuanku* (His

Majesty commands your presence before him)." The *Yang Di-Pertuan Muda* then goes in and performs the ceremonial *menjunjong duli,* and comes out again immediately he finishes. Then the *bentara* comes out again and calls out — this time, standing up — the names of the rest of the princes, ministers, *dato'* and all titled officials, who are to come in, one after another, to make obeisance to the newly-proclaimed *Yang Di-Pertuan Besar.*

(e) At the end of the *menjunjong duli* ceremony, the *Nobat* changes to the tune *"Arak-Arak",* and the gun is again fired in salute when the *Yang Di-Pertuan Besar* is taken in procession, in the same manner as before, back to the *Istana* for *santap nasi adap-adapan* (royal eating ceremony). Meanwhile, in the *Balairong,* all sit down to a sumptuous curry and rice feast, and alms (money, gold and silver) are widely distributed to the poor, needy, orphans, and disabled.

15. DRESS REGULATIONS FOR THOSE INSIDE THE PERDALAMAN (THE ROYAL COMPOUND) DURING THE INSTALLATION CEREMONY

(a) Men are not allowed inside if they are wearing: *baju khas* (specially made high-collar *baju*); *mopon* buttons (a type of filigree button, specially made for certain royal personages); *baju* inside or under the *sarong* with *keris* pointing towards the back. They are permitted to wear a belt or *pending,* but the *baju* must be outside the *sarong* with the *keris* pointing towards the front. It is also permissible to wear patterned silk.

(b) Women are not permitted to wear *baju takua* (special long *baju* with narrow sleeves); sleeve-buttons worn lengthwise; blouse-buttons *berjajar* (in a row); *baju* of patterned silk; *baju* of *kain antelas* (satin); *baju berantai* (chain-patterned); *sarong* without *kepala* (front section of different design); white chain-patterned *sarong*; *chita* (cotton fabric) and cloth with patterns. But women without titles may wear sleeve-buttons *berlengkong* (curved); white head-covers; silk and *mastuli* (cloth fabric of heavy silk); *sarong* with gold-threaded *kepala;* Bugis, hand-woven Palembang or *batek sarong;* and they may also wear *pending.*

(c) *Anak2 raja perempuan* (princesses) should all wear *baju pandak* (short *baju*); and they may wear silk *baju* without pattern; *baju* of *kain telepok* (fabric adorned with tinsel) unpatterned; and *kain berantai* as long as it is not white. But they may not wear sleeve-buttons lengthwise, nor may they wear flowered, knitted, or lacy head-covers.

(d) As soon as the *anak2 raja perempuan* (princesses) arrive at the *tela* door, they must take off their *kain kelumbong atas* (*sarong* used as a hood and shawl), and hand them over to their maids, as it is not permissible for the ladies to carry them around or to leave them draped around their shoulders.

NOTE:
These dress regulations are only in force within the royal precincts.

## BERIKRAR SETIA (THE OATH OF LOYALTY)

(*This oath is taken by the Sultan during the Tabal ceremony, and also on other occasions, for example, the proclamation of a new monarch.*)

The following is the procedure:

1. The *Balairong* is made ready, suitably arranged and decorated, as is usual for any royal or state ceremony.

2. The seat of the *Yang Di-Pertuan Besar* or *Sultan* is placed at the head of the *Balairong* (or *Seri Balai* as it is formally called).

3. First, all those required to attend the ceremony are admitted.

4. When they have taken their places, the articles required for use in the ceremony are brought in:

(i) One bowl of pure water
(ii) The Quran Al-Kareem
(iii) The Letter of Oath
(iv) The Royal Seal
(v) Two candle-stands with lighted candles.

These are placed in their proper order close to the *Singgahsana* (throne). All *penjawat* in attendance wear *tetampan* and sit in line on the right and left sides of the *Singgahsana*.

5. Then enter the *Yang Di-Pertuan Muda* and other princes, with the ministers and *dato'* as well as other high-ranking officials of the State. They take their alloted places on the *Balai* or platforms immediately facing the *Singgahsana*.

6. When everything is in order, the *Yang Di-Pertuan Besar* arrives, accompanied by his *penjawat*. His arrival is acclaimed by simultaneous shouts of *"Daulat Tuanku"* from all in the *Balairong*. The *Sultan* sits on the *Singgahsana* while all the *penjawat* accompanying him sit in line behind him.

7. Then the *bentara* (herald) comes forward and, after making the usual obeisance (*menyembah*) takes up the Letter of Oath and reads it in a very clear and loud voice. During the reading, the *Yang Di-Pertuan Besar* is to put both his hands on the Quran — just once and briefly — as a sign that he has truly and solemnly taken the oath.

8. After the reading of the Letter of Oath, the *Nobat* plays and those present in the *Balai*, led by the *Yang Di-Pertuan Muda*, make obeisance (*Menjunjong-Duli*), with the *Nobat* playing the tune *"Ibrahim Khalilullah"*.

9. The *Nobat* stops playing immediately the *Menjunjong-Duli* ends, and a salute of sixteen guns is fired.

10. After the last shot of the gun, the *Yang Di-Pertuan Besar* leaves the *Balairong* to return to the *Istana* with all his retinue, followed by all the others in the *Balai*.

11. After accompanying the *Yang Di-Pertuan Besar* to the *Istana*, all the princes, ministers and *dato'* as well as the officials, return to the *Balairong* to partake of the *jamuan* that has been prepared for the occasion. The *Yang Di-Pertuan Muda* is usually entertained in the *Istana*.

CHAPTER FIVE

# DEMISE AND FUNERAL OF A RULING MONARCH

1. DEMISE AND MOURNING

WHEN a ruling *Sultan* dies, the sorrowful event is immediately made known to the public, and at the same time the period of mourning is proclaimed to start immediately. The following regulations for the royal mourning are usually adopted:

  (i) Mourning for a *Sultan* or *Yang Di-Pertuan Besar* is for a period of one hundred days.

 (ii) Mourning for a *Yang Di-Pertuan Muda* or *Putera Mahkota* is for a period of forty days.

(iii) Mourning for a *Bendahara* is for fourteen days.

The modes of mourning adopted are as follows:

 (a) For the male *ra'ayat*, whether of royal descent or otherwise, *baju* and *seluar* (trousers) with *sarong* of black colour and white *tengkolok* or *tanjak* (olden-day Malay head-gear). Nowadays because of changed conditions, it is permissible to wear a cap (*songkok*), with a strip of white cloth or ribbon about two inches wide round the bottom edge of the *songkok*. Officials and fighting men (*hulubalang pahlawan*) with arms or weapons, such as swords, *keris*, spears or the like, are also to have a mourning band of white cloth or ribbon tied to the handles of the weapons. All the *pawai* (articles of the royal regalia) must have strips of white tied to them. The *Nobat* observes mourning by **wrapping the two** *gendang* **and the** two *nengkara* with white cloth.

(b) For women, black *baju* and *sarong* with white *selendang* or *kain tudong kepala*.

## 2. THE ROYAL LYING-IN-STATE IN THE ISTANA

When it is ready, the royal body in its coffin is carried and placed on a *peterakna* in the court of the *Istana* where it is to lie in state before interment. The coffin on the *peterakna* is curtained with yellow silk and on the top are placed the Crown and Sword of State of the late *Sultan*. The coffin is guarded day and night by *penjawat* and guards in rotation, under the leadership of the

*Penghulu Istana*. It is also arranged that four to six *haji* at a time are to read the Quran throughout the day and night during the lying-in-state of the royal remains.

3. **PROCEDURE FOR THE PAYING OF RESPECTS BY MEMBERS OF THE PUBLIC**

All *kerabat* (close relatives of the late Sultan), *dato'*, officials of the State, and members of the public of both sexes and of all nationalities, may pay their last homage to the deceased *Sultan* while his body is lying in state before interment. The times usually fixed for such visits are:
   (a) During the day: from 8 a.m. to 5 p.m.
   (b) In the evening: from 7 p.m. to 9 or 10 p.m.

The number of visitors allowed at each visit is in accordance with regulations previously determined. At all times there is one high-ranking official of the State taking his turn to be on duty at the *Istana*, to advise and help the visitors whenever required.

4. **ARRANGEMENTS ON THE DAY OF THE ROYAL FUNERAL**

One hour before the scheduled departure of the royal cortège from the *Istana*, a gun is fired in announcement to the public.

The following *pawai* (articles of the royal regalia) and their bearers are kept in readiness before the start of the royal funeral procession to the the *Makam* (Mausoleum):

(i) Sixteen payong ubor-ubo (royal ceremonial umbrellas) — eight yellow and eight white, with their bearers, in mourning, wearing yellow *baju* and white *seluar* and *sarong*

(ii) Sixteen *Lembing* (Spears) and bearers

(iii) Sixteen *Pebaran* (Incense-burners) and bearers

(iv) Sixteen *Kaki-dian* complete with *dian* (candle-stands with candles) and bearers

(v) Sixteen *Kain-Dukong* (ceremonial neck-cloths) and bearers.

All the above bearers are to be youths of gentle birth, each wearing *baju*, *seluar* and *sarong* of black.

Also in mourning are one hundred male bearers of the royal *Usongan* (hammock litter), made up of *penghulu* of *mukim* of the country, all wearing uniform dress of yellow *baju*, white *seluar* and *sarong*. With the royal coffin on the *Usongan* are *penjawat* carrying the following articles:

(i) One *Talqin* mat (a mat on which the reader of the exhortation to the dead sits)

(ii) Eight *ambur* or *embat* (rose-water sprinklers)

(iii) Two jugs or bottles of *Talqin* water (water, mixed with sandalwood powder for sprinkling or pouring over the grave)

(iv) Two bottles of rose-water, and two special *penjawat*.

Each of the above bearers is dressed in black and white, and wears a *tetampan* dangling from his left shoulder.

On the royal coffin are placed the royal Crown and Sword of State of the late monarch.

5. PROCLAMATION OF THE ACCESSION OF THE NEW RULER

On the same day and before the interment of the royal remains, the ceremony for the proclamation of the new monarch is held in the *Balairong Seri* before all the *anak2 raja, dato'*, officials, and *hamba-ra'ayat* (members of the public). In one specially allotted section of the *Balai* are *penjawat* of the royal regalia, and in another section is the band of the *Nobat* in full strength and in mourning.

Promptly at the appointed hour the *Yang Di-Pertuan Muda* or *Putera Mahkota*, Heir Apparent to the throne of the country, escorted by the Prime Minister, ministers and high-ranking officials of the State, is led to the *Balairong Seri,* and enthroned on the *perterakna* of the *Singgahsana.* The arrival of His Royal Highness is proclaimed and received with high ovation and the beating of the *Nobat.* When all the arrangements are completed and all are in their rightful places, the *Nobat* ceases to play. The Prime Minister then comes forward in a most respectful manner and announces the necessity of appointing His Royal Highness to take the place of *Almarhum,* the deceased monarch, and asks for the approval of the *ra'ayat.* This is immediately answered by those present saying in one voice *"Suka"* (a word showing agreement). The Prime Minister then turns to His Royal Highness and begins to read the proclamation of the accession of His Royal Highness to the throne as *Sultan* and *Yang Di-Pertuan Besar* of the country. After the proclamation, the *Dato' Bentara Dalam* (the Lord Chamberlain) cries *"Daulat Tuanku"* three times. The rest of the assembly present, inside and outside the *Balai,* repeat the cry with one voice, and immediately after follows the beating of the *Nobat* and the raising of the Royal Standard from half-mast to full-mast, where it is left until the ceremony is terminated by the State *Mufti* reading the *do'a selamat* (prayer for blessing). The *Yang Maha Mulia,* the new monarch, replies in a clear voice, accepting the appointment and undertaking to do his duties sincerely and honestly towards his country and his people, in full obedience and loyalty to the bidding of Allah. The ceremony is terminated by all those present, inside and outside the *Balai*, again proclaiming, with one accord, *"Daulat Tuanku"* three times, the *Mufti* reading the *do'a selamat*, the *Nobat* beating its final tune, and the firing of a salute of twenty-one guns.

## 6. PROCESSION OF THE ROYAL FUNERAL TO THE MAKAM

Immediately after the end of the ceremony of proclamation, the royal coffin is taken on the *Usongan* in procession from the *Istana* to the *Makam* (Mausoleum). All down the middle of the roads to the *Makam*, along which the royal funeral procession is to pass, is spread yellow cloth, three to four feet wide, called *kain Puadai* and along both sides of the roads are stretched ropes encased in yellow cloth.

The order of the procession is as follows:
  (a) Heading the royal procession walks the *Dato' Birachana* (master of Royal Ceremonies and Processions), in *isti'adat* dress and in mourning.
  (b) Next comes the *Nobat* in full ceremonial dress and in mourning.
  (c) A battalion or group of *hulubalang*

*pahlawan* (fighting men), in full dress and in mourning follows.

(d) Sixteen officers in ceremonial dress and in mourning, bearing *lembing* or *tombak* (spears).

(e) Sixteen officers bearing *pebaran* (incense-burners).

(f) A group of sixteen bearers of candle-stands (complete with candles).

(g) The royal regalia bearers.

(h) Then comes the *Usongan* of the royal remains with a group of sixteen *penjawat2 Kain-Dukong* walking immediately behind.

(i) Then comes *Duli Yang Maha Mulia*, the newly proclaimed *Sultan*, with *Sultan* of other countries, governors, and high dignitaries of foreign countries.

(j) *Anak2 raja, dato'* and high-ranking officials of the State come next.

(k) Then come old people of honoured families and of gentle birth, and well-known people of other nationalities.

(l) Lastly follow the general public.

7. REGULATIONS ON ARRIVAL AT THE MAKAM

On the arrival of the royal procession at the gate of the *Makam*, the band of the *Nobat* stops and remains standing in its proper ceremonial order on one side, close to the door of the *Makam* building. The battalion of *hulubalang pahlawan* (fighting men) stops and lines up on the right and left sides of the road leading to the *Makam* building.

As soon as the royal coffin is borne in, passing between their lines, the usual homage (bowing and reading the Quran) is paid by them, and the *Nobat* immediaely beats its appropriate tune.

The *penjawat* and regalia bearers enter the *Makam* house and stand in line on the right and left sides of the building. All the *penjawat* and the rest of the bearers are supervised by the *Penghulu Isti'adat*.

All those accompanying the royal funeral, who are either royalty, *tuan2 syed*, *dato* officials of the country, dignitaries of other countries or close friends of the late *Sultan*, are admitted into the *Makam* building and placed at positions previously determined in accordance with their rank and title. The rest of the crowd remain outside.

The royal coffin is taken down from the litter by *Duli Yang Maha Mulia*, the newly proclaimed *Sultan*, close *kerabat* (relations) of the late monarch and the *dato'* and placed on a smaller litter and carried into the *Makam* to a place where the State *Mufti* leads the reading of the *Al-Fatehah* over the royal remains. After this the royal coffin is conveyed to and lowered into the grave, in which a few *dato'* and very close relations help the State *Imam* to arrange the royal remains, as required by Islam, before the grave is filled in.

When all is done and the royal grave filled in and made ready for the reading of the *Talqin* (exhortation to the dead), the Chief *Kadhi* of the State comes forward and sits on the *Talqin* mat, already spread by the side of the grave. After the bearer of the *Talqin* water has sprinkled all of it over the grave, the Chief *Kadhi* reads the *Talqin*. The *Mufti* of State then leads the crowd in *tahlil* (reading certain rites for the soul of the dead) that ends with a *do'a selamat* and distribution of alms to the poor and needy. The royal interment thus ends and the crowd disperses.

*PLEASE NOTE:*

*Almost all the above regulations, arrangements and articles mentioned in this chapter, are those adopted and used in the Isti'adat Permakaman (Royal Funeral and Interment) of the Duli Yang Maha Mulia Almarhum Sultan Abu Bakar of Johore — may Allah bless his soul — that took place in Johore Bahru on the 17th day of Ra'alawal, 1313 (7th day of September, 1895).*

**PLATES**

Plate 1. TONGKAT PENGHULU ISTANA

    Ceremonial Staff for Palace Penghulu.
    A for Chief Penghulu,
    B & C for his deputies.

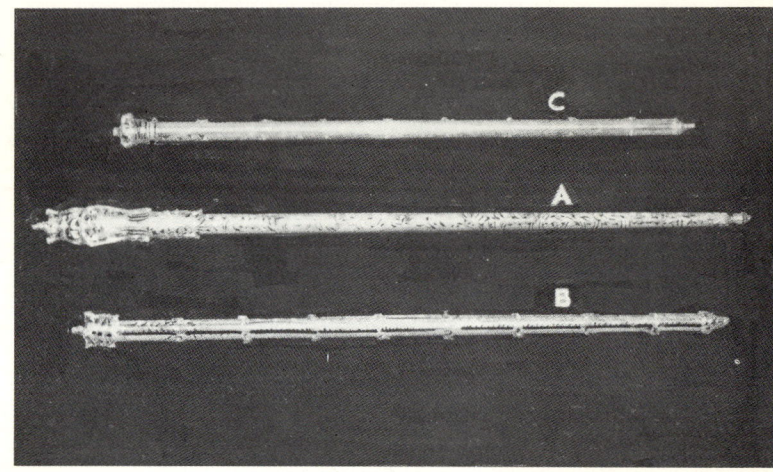

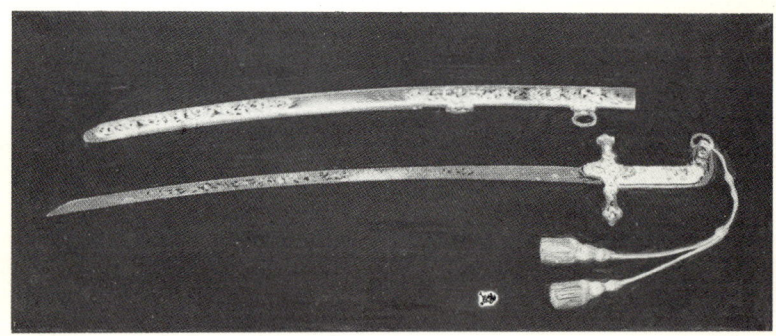

Plate 2. PEDANG KERAJAAN
    Sword of State.

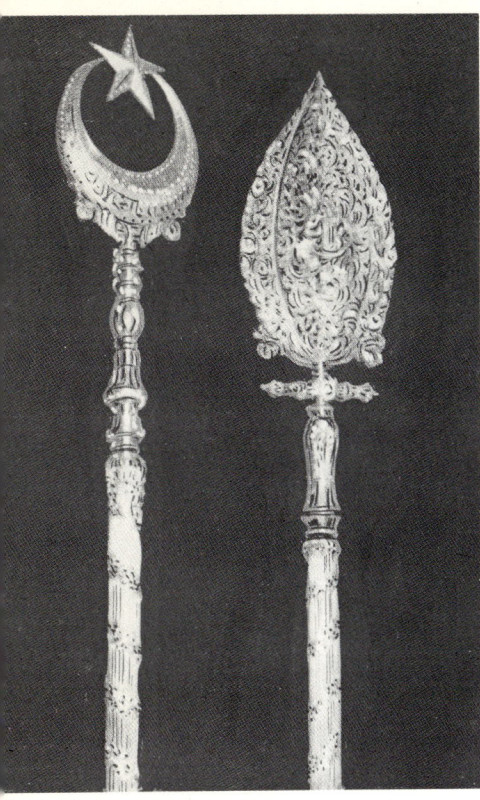

Plate 3.

CHOGAN

Standard.

*Left*: Chogan Negara or Kerajaan (State)
*Right*: Chogan Ugama. (Religion)

Plate 4.

PEDANG KERAJAAN

Sword of State.

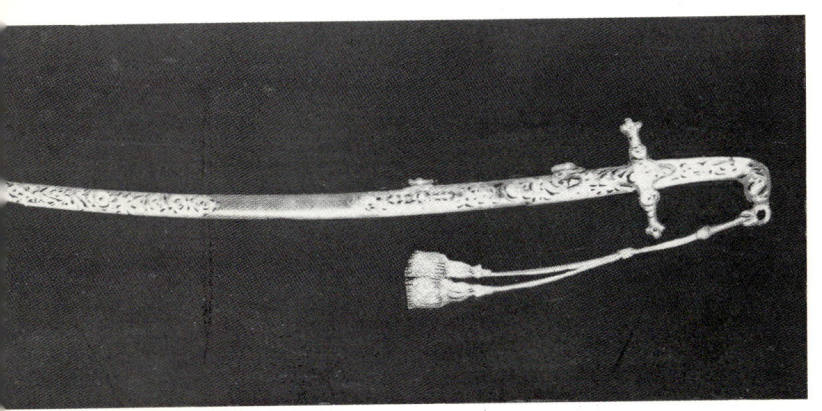

Plate 5.

WALI

Ceremonial shoulder-cloth *white* in colour, worn on *right* shoulder.

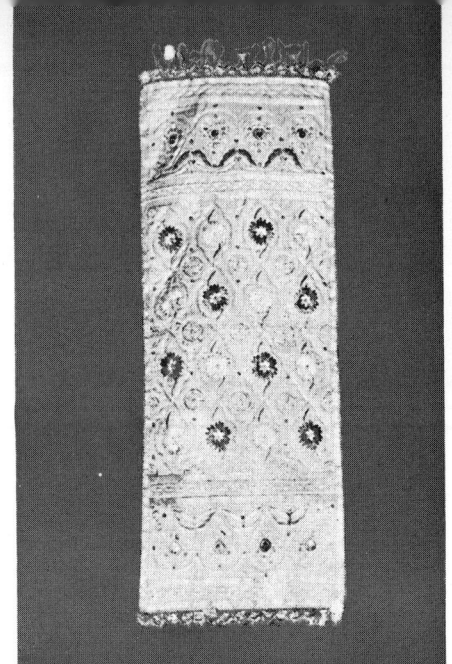

Plate 6.

SELENDANG

Ceremonial sash, worn by Lembing-, Tombak-, and other bearers in royal ceremonies or processions.

Plate 7.

KAIN-DUKONG

Ceremonial cloth worn dangling down from the neck.

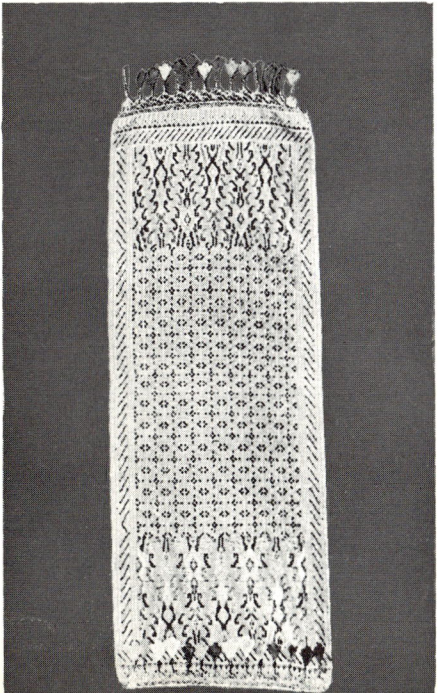

Plate 8.

TETAMPAN

Ceremonial shoulder-cloth, *yellow* in colour worn on the *left* shoulder.

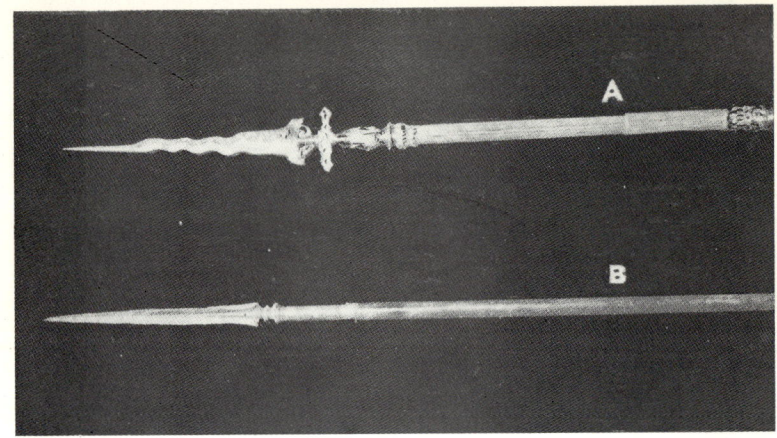

Plate 9. LEMBING TOMBAK

    A. Lembing Kerajaan
       Spear with ridged blade
    B. Tombak Biasa
       Spear with straight blade

     (both used in Royal ceremonies).

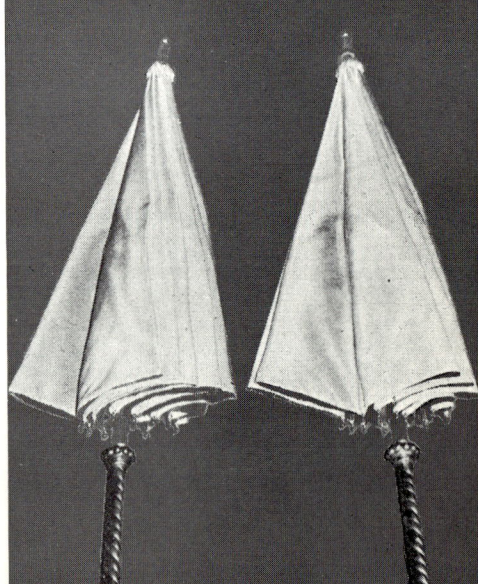

Plate 10. PAYONG UBOR-UBOR Royal ceremonial umbrellas.

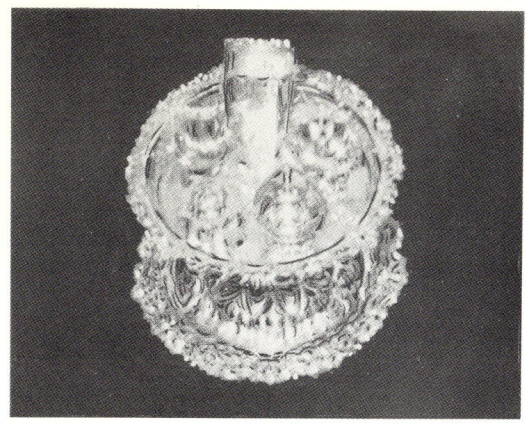

Plate 11.
PUAN
Caddy-shaped large betel-bowl usually of silver.

Plate 12. TEPAK SIREH
*Sireh*-box of Palembang type.

Plate 13.
ENGKU MAI

APPENDIX

## A BRIEF BIOGRAPHY OF
## ENGKU MAI

RAJA MAIMUNAH BINTI RAJA HASSAN ibni Almarhum Raja Abdullah (*Tengku Panglima Besar*, son-in-law to Almarhum Sultan Muhammad, who ruled Negri Selangor from 1826-1856) is better known as Engku Mai, and is believed to be the oldest descendant of royalty living in Selangor (and possibly in the Malay Peninsula) today. At present she lives in Jalan Siantan, Kampong Raja Uda, Port Swettenham, Klang, Selangor.

Engku Mai was born at Kuala Linggi, Malacca, but was brought up in both Rhio and Klang, between which she went to and fro very often.

She cannot remember the exact date of her birth, but can remember definitely that she was fifteen years old when the "Battle of Raja Mahdi" started in Selangor. Thus she is not less than one hundred and twenty years old (reckoning by the Islamic Calendar). She grew up in the *Istana* of both the *Yang Di-Pertuan Besar* of Rhio and of the *Sultan* of Selangor. She is, therefore, very conversant with the old '*adat isti'adat* of the Royal households of Rhio and Selangor.

Engku Mai was first married to Raja Ali bin Raja Muhammad and after his death she married Tengku Kudin. At the time the author interviewed her, she had seventy-two great-grand-children, and three great-great-grand-children. In spite of her advanced age, and except for the loss of her sight, she was in good health, and she was in full possession of her mental faculties. She talked clearly and was in good spirits all through the interview.

May the blessing of Allah be always upon her.